4

Ingredients

with

GOURMET
GARDEN®
HERBS & SPICES

GOURMET
GARDEN®
HERBS & SPICES

Botanical Food Company Pty Ltd
Palmwoods, QLD 4555
Australia

G.G. (Europe) Ltd.
Rhosili Rd, Brackmills,
Northampton UK
NN4 7AN
www.gourmetgarden.com

Ingredients

4 Ingredients
PO Box 400
Caloundra QLD 4551
Australia

ABN: 19 307 118 068

www.4ingredients.co.uk
www.4ingredients.com.au
info@4ingredients.com.au

Published by 4 Ingredients, September 2010

Cover & Formatting: Allure Creative, www.allurecreative.com.au
Printing & Binding: Clays Ltd, UK 01986 893 211

AUS Distributor: Simon & Schuster (02) 9983 6600
NZ Distributor: Random House (09) 444 7197
UK Distributor: Simon & Schuster UK Ltd 020 7316 1900

ISBN: 932-8-327-00149-6

Foreword

At 4 Ingredients we are always looking for products, practices and ideas to help reduce time and money spent in the kitchen but not compromise flavour.

When it comes to cooking, we believe the most important ingredient in any recipe is FLAVOUR! It doesn't matter how many ingredients it contains, be it 4 or 40, if you go to the effort of cooking something, you want the end result to be flavoursome. And this is where our love affair with Gourmet Garden began … It made our lives in the kitchen easier and tastier.

Fresh herbs and spices really make a difference to the flavour and quality of a meal, but during the week it's hard to find time to buy or prepare them. A fabulous solution for all busy cooks who don't want to miss out on flavour is Gourmet Garden herbs and spices. What we love most about these products are:

♥ They are simply washed, chopped, blended and packed fresh. They really are fresh herbs made easy for everyday cooking

♥ They retain their colour, aroma, texture and most importantly their flavour

♥ They contain no artificial flavours or colours and they last for 3 months in the fridge, so there's no wastage

♥ They are made from organically grown Australian herbs and are based on the beautiful Sunshine Coast, QLD Australia — just as we are!

There are over 15 Gourmet Garden products and what surprised us when cooking, creating and compiling this book was the sheer variety of dishes both sweet and savoury that can be created with only 4 Ingredients; Chocolate Basil Ganache, Rosemary Caramel Tarts, Herbal & Healthy fruit salads, Mascarpone & Coriander Chicken, Apricot & Mint Fish and *soooo* many more.

Creating this book for Gourmet Garden was a sensational learning experience for us; we know you will enjoy it too!

Happy Herbal Cooking

Kim & Rachael

GOURMET GARDEN®

HERBS & SPICES

Fresh Made Easy™

Basil	A Gourmet Garden Basil tube is equivalent to 3 bunches of fresh basil.
	Basil is a good source of antioxidants and contains more antioxidants per serve than most vegetables and many fruits, so adding just a little basil to your meals can also give your diet an antioxidant boost. Simply add a little or a lot depending on your taste.
Chilli	A Gourmet Garden Chilli tube is equivalent to 5 large fresh chillies.
	Chilli is best added at the beginning of the cooking process to allow its flavour to permeate your dish. Chilli is also a source of antioxidants so adding it to your cooking can have health benefits too. Gourmet Garden Chilli is available in Hot and Mild, so depending on your taste, simply add a little or a lot.
Chives	A Gourmet Garden Chives tube is equivalent to 3 bunches of fresh chives.
	Chives are one of the milder herbs and has an onion-like flavour with a hint of garlic, helping to boost the flavour, colour and aroma of a wide variety of dishes. Chives cannot withstand cooking and so is best added just before serving. Chives are a source of antioxidants so you can also boost your daily antioxidant intake by adding just a small amount to your meal.
Coriander	A Gourmet Garden Coriander tube is equivalent to 3 bunches of fresh coriander.
	Coriander is one of the world's most popular herbs, with its distinctive, pungent earthy taste similar to a blend of lemon and sage. Coriander's flavour can be lost when cooked, so be sure to add it near the end of cooking your meal. The volatile oil in Coriander can make it very strong to some palates, so add according to your taste.
Dill	A Gourmet Garden Dill tube is equivalent to 3 bunches of fresh dill.
	Known for its crisp grassy taste and rich aroma, dill is a perfect seasoning for seafood. Dill also works great with cheese, eggs and cream sauces or added to your favourite salad dressing.
Garlic	A Gourmet Garden Garlic tube is equivalent to 23 cloves of fresh garlic.
	Garlic's unique taste lends itself to almost every cuisine from Asian and Indian to Italian and Mexican. Garlic is extremely versatile and is found in many stir fries, pastas and curries. From pizza to poultry, garlic is great with most foods. Garlic is best added at the beginning of the cooking process to allow its flavour to transform your dish. Gourmet Garden Garlic is available in chunky and regular garlic.
Ginger	A Gourmet Garden Ginger tube is equivalent to 21 pieces of fresh ginger.
	Ginger is best added at the beginning of the cooking process to allow its flavour to transform your dish. Ginger is great for adding spice to fish, seafood, poultry, meat, vegetable and noodle dishes.

Italian Herbs	A Gourmet Garden Italian Herbs tube is equivalent to 3 bunches of fresh herbs.
	Gourmet Garden Italian Herbs are perfect in a wide range of both traditional and modern dishes including pasta, pizza, bruschetta, salad, soups, veal and chicken. Italian Herbs combines a unique blend of Oregano, Basil, Marjoram, Thyme, Parsley and Rosemary.
Lemon Grass	A Gourmet Garden Lemon Grass tube is equivalent to 6 stalks of fresh lemon grass.
	Originally from India, lemon grass is known for the fresh, lemon-like flavour and rose hinted fragrance it brings to many dishes, especially Thai and Vietnamese cuisine. Additionally, lemon grass is a good source of antioxidants so adding just a little to your meal can help boost your immune system and maximize your wellbeing. Lemon grass has previously been used as a traditional remedy for infection and fever.
Mint	A Gourmet Garden Mint tube is equivalent to 3 bunches of fresh mint.
	To preserve its flavour and colour, add mint at the end of your cooking. Studies show that Mint is a rich source of antioxidants and contains more antioxidants per serve than most vegetables and many fruits. So adding just a little mint to an array of dishes, such as sauces and dips can give your diet an antioxidant boost.
Oregano	A Gourmet Garden Oregano tube is equivalent to 3 bunches of fresh oregano.
	Originally from Greece and Italy, Oregano is perfect in pizzas, pasta sauces, marinades and salad dressings and is also great with grilled fish, kebabs and roast meat. Oregano compliments many ingredients, such as chilli, garlic and tomato, especially when stirred into hot vegetable dishes or tomato-based soups. Add oregano at the end of your cooking to maintain its flavour and aroma.
Parsley	A Gourmet Garden Parsley tube is equivalent to 3 bunches of fresh parsley.
	Parsley is a very versatile herb with its light, fresh scent and flavour and is used in many European, Middle Eastern and Mediterranean dishes. Parsley is the perfect addition to a wide range of dishes including soups, stews, meat, poultry, egg dishes, potatoes, salads and stuffing. Add parsley at the end of cooking to maintain its flavour and colour. Adding parsley to your meal is also an ideal way to boost your antioxidant intake.
Rosemary	A Gourmet Garden Rosemary tube is equivalent to 17 sprigs of fresh rosemary.
	Part of the mint family and originally from the Mediterranean, Rosemary is perfect rubbed on lamb, pork or chicken before barbequing or roasting. Studies show that Rosemary is a rich source of antioxidants and contains more antioxidants per serve than most vegetables and many fruits. So adding just a little Rosemary to your meals can give you an antioxidant boost.

Note: *If some Gourmet Garden products are not available in your local supermarket please feel free to replace with fresh herbs and spices.*

1 tbs. Gourmet Garden = 1 tbs. fresh chopped herbs & spices.

Visit **www.gourmetgarden.com** for hundreds of quick and delicious recipes.

Guide to Weights & Measures

A big fancy conversion table is not required,
as all you need to make the recipes within 4 Ingredients are:

1 teaspoon (1 tsp.)
1 tablespoon (1 tbs.)
1 cup (250ml)
or the following:

Product	Grams per Cup	Product	Grams per Cup
Almond Meal	170	Nuts–Pecans	120
BBQ Sauce	280	Nuts–Pine nuts	160
Butter	230	Nuts–Pistachios	120
Basil Pesto	260	Nuts–Walnuts	100
Breadcrumbs	130	Pasta (dried)	75
Brown sugar, packed	220	Pasta Sauce	175
Caster sugar	200	Peanut butter	260
Cheese	100	Popcorn	40
Chutney	300	Raisins	170
Cornflakes	120	Rice	185
Cornflour	120	Rice bubbles	80
Desiccated Coconut	120	Rolled oats	100
Dried apricots	160	Salsa	175
Dried mixed fruit	170	Self raising flour	175
Flour–Plain	175	Sour cream	320
Flour–Self Raising	175	Sultanas	170
Honey	320	Sugar–White	220
Icing Sugar	120	Sugar–Raw	200
Jam	320	Sweet chilli sauce	320
Maple Syrup	240	Tandoori paste	225
Mayonnaise	260	Tomato paste	260
Natural Muesli	110	Tomato Sauce	280
Nuts–Almonds	160	Yoghurt	250

Abbreviations Used

Gram	g
Kilogram	kg
Millilitre	ml
Litre	ltr

Oven Temperature Guide

Making friends with your oven really helps when cooking. Basically the Celsius temperature is about half the Fahrenheit temperature.

Most ovens these days offer the option to bake or fan bake (amongst others); as a rule, having the fan-assisted option will greatly increase the temperature in your oven and will shorten cooking times.

Our recipes have been compiled assuming a static conventional oven (non fan-forced) unless otherwise stated. If however your oven is fan forced as a general rule of thumb, conventional cooking temperatures are reduced by 20°C (this may vary between models). So if the recipe reads bake for 1 hour at 200°C that will be 1 hour at 180°C fan-forced.

Here's some help:

	Slow	Slow	Mod	Mod	Mod hot	Mod hot	Hot	Hot	Very hot
Fahrenheit	275	300	325	350	375	400	425	450	475
Celsius	140	150	165	180	190	200	220	230	240
Gas Mark	1	2	3	4	5	6	7	8	9

4 Ingredients Titles

4 Ingredients

The initial book in the blockbuster series
4 Ingredients was printed against trade advice.
2,000 books "that were never going to sell" have
now sold over 2.5 MILLION copies. If you are
a busy person, on a budget, moved out of home,
are travelling or do not have a lot of space for
a full pantry, or you simply haven't had time to
buy groceries, then this is the book for you!

4 Ingredients 2

Kim and Rachael wrote 4 ingredients because it
was a book they needed. They now bring you 4
Ingredients 2 because it was a book YOU wanted!
There are over 400 new recipes that were collected
at events, signings, expos and online from all
around the world. This is a book for busy people
who want fantastic food – fast!

4 Ingredients Gluten Free

You may think that living on a gluten free diet
means living on a taste free diet, but this book
proves this is far from the truth! With gluten
intolerances now affecting 1 in 20 people, there has
never been a better time to learn about gluten free
cooking. You will be AMAZED what can be cooked
without gluten and with just 4 ingredients.

4 Ingredients Fast Fresh & Healthy

Kim and Rachael have teamed up with world
famous mind-body expert, Deepak Chopra to
create the most anticipated book in the series so
far. This exciting cookbook shows you how to take
4 ingredients, combine them and make spectacular
recipes that are DELICIOUS using fresh, nutrient
rich ingredients for a healthier mind and body.

www.4ingredients.co.uk
www.4ingredients.com.au

Table of Contents

Foreword 3

Fresh Made Easy 4

    Guide to weights & measures 6

    4 Ingredients Titles 8

Table of Contents 9

Breakfasts 11

Dips 18

Condiments 24

Cocktail Food 31

Morning & Afternoon Teas.......................................38

Light Meals & Lunches 44

Sides...51

    Salads 51

    Potato 56

    Vegetables 62

Mains 69

    Beef 69

    Chicken..75

    Fish & Seafood 81

    Lamb..89

    Pasta 94

    Pork...101

    Vegetarian 106

Desserts..113

For the Children 120

Drinks 130

Herbs & Spices Matched & Married 135

Biography — Kim McCosker.......................................136

Biography — Rachael Bermingham.............................137

Bibliography 138

Index...140

Breakfasts

*Gourmet Garden Herbs & Spices are picked at their peak,
then washed, chopped, blended and sealed in clever tubes
to capture their fresh flavour and antioxidants.
It's like having a fresh herb and spice garden in your
refrigerator all year round!*

Fresh Made Easy™

Breakfast Tomatoes with Chives

MAKES 4

- *4 medium, firm tomatoes*
- *2 tbs. Gourmet Garden Chives*
- *4 eggs*
- *½ cup grated cheese*

Preheat oven to 180°C. Line a baking tray with baking paper. Cut half a 1cm slice from top of each tomato, scoop out 75% of the pulp, leaving shell intact. Place tomatoes upside down on paper towels and drain for 5 minutes. Place tomatoes right side up on tray, rub inside with chives and season with sea salt and pepper. Break an egg into each tomato. Sprinkle evenly with cheese and bake for 20–25 minutes or until the eggs are set.

Tip: Chives are so versatile that they add flavour to many savoury dishes. Use in salads, sauces, egg, potato, and yoghurt dishes. Chives are also a great companion for cheese dishes.

Ham, Basil & Feta Scrambled Eggs

SERVES 2

- 4 eggs, lightly beaten
- ½ cup diced ham
- ¼ cup crumbled feta cheese
- 1 tsp. Gourmet Garden Basil

Place a non-stick fry pan over medium heat. Place the lightly beaten eggs in a bowl; add in ham, feta, basil and season. Pour the mixture in the pan and cook, stirring occasionally for 5 minutes or until firm.

Herbed Cream Cheese Omelette

SERVES 4

- 115g cream cheese, softened
- 2 tsp. Gourmet Garden Coriander
- 3 tbs. (45g) butter
- 8 eggs

Mix cream cheese and coriander in a bowl adding salt and pepper. Heat a quarter of the butter in a non-stick fry pan over medium/high heat. When bubbling, swirl to coat the entire base. Beat two of the eggs and pour into pan then lower the heat. After 1 minute, dab a quarter of the herbed cream cheese along the middle of the omelette. When the omelette is just set, fold in half and continue cooking for 30 seconds. Slide onto a serving plate. Serve immediately and make three more omelettes the same way.

Tip: Coriander's flavour can be lost when cooked, so be sure to add it near the end of cooking your meal.

Fluffy Scrambled Eggs with Chives

SERVES 4

- 8 eggs
- 1 tsp. Gourmet Garden Chives
- 145ml evaporated milk
- 2 tbs. (30g) butter

In a bowl, whisk the eggs, chives and milk until combined. In a frying pan, heat butter until hot. Add egg mixture and cook, stirring over a medium heat until eggs are completely set. Season with sea salt and pepper.

Fact: Gourmet Garden Chives are grown without the use of artificial pesticides, herbicides or fertilisers.

Garlic Hash Browns

MAKES 10

- 4 large potatoes
- 1 tsp. Gourmet Garden Garlic
- 1 egg, lightly whisked
- ⅓ cup (80ml) olive oil

Peel and grate potatoes and put into a large bowl. Squeeze out excess juice. Add garlic and egg and stir through potatoes. Stir in a good pinch of salt. Add oil to fry pan and heat until very hot. Add heaped dessert spoonfuls of potato mixture to pan. Fry for 3 minutes and gently turn, cook other side for 2–3 minutes or until golden brown. These are great for breakfast, lunch or dinner.

Fact: Make sure you cook these without delay as the grated potato discolours rapidly.

Ginger Pancakes

MAKES 4

Our children love these.

- 1 cup (175g) self raising flour
- 1 egg
- 1 cup (250ml) milk
- ½ tsp. Gourmet Garden Ginger

Sift flour, add egg and a pinch of salt. Beat, gradually adding milk until thick and smooth. Add ginger and lightly mix. Heat non-stick frying pan. Pour desired quantity into pan, cook until bubbling on top and then flip.

Optional: Serve with maple syrup, lemon juice and sugar, honey or stewed fruits.

Ginger & Tomato Jam

- 3 kg ripe tomatoes
- 2 kg sugar
- 4 lemons, juiced
- 2 tbs. Gourmet Garden Ginger

Skin tomatoes by scalding for a few minutes in boiling water, place in a large saucepan with sugar, lemon juice, finely shredded rind and ginger. Boil rapidly until jam sets when tested. Bottle.

Hint: If making jam be sure that your jars are heated to seal well To test if jam is done, remove a teaspoon of the liquid and place on a very cold saucer and observe whether it appears to be jam-like in consistency as it cools. (See: Marmalade for helpful tips).

Individual Egg Bakes

SERVES 8

- *8 bacon rashers*
- *½ cup (140g) tomato or BBQ sauce*
- *8 eggs*
- *2 tsp. Gourmet Garden Parsley*

Partially cook bacon in fry pan until half done. Drain on paper towel. Line an 8 hole muffin tray with muffin papers and then line each with a rasher of bacon. Mix together tomato sauce and parsley then use a knife to smooth tomato sauce around each slice of bacon. Break one egg into each cup and season with sea salt and pepper. Place muffin tray in a 200°C oven and bake for 18–20 minutes or until eggs are cooked. Let stand for 2 minutes then lift eggs out of cups onto a serving platter, removing the paper. Spoon sauce left in the muffin cups over eggs and serve.

Tip: Parsley is not a dominant herb so adding it to dishes enhances the flavour of the food rather than giving them the flavour of the herb. It softens the strong odour of vegetables such as garlic and onions and combines well with other herbs ... "Parsley, sage, rosemary, and thyme" are words in a once popular song for a reason!

Mango Mint Smoothie

SERVES 1

Breakfast on the Goooo ... Delicious!

- *1 ripe mango, cubed*
- *4 large ripe strawberries, hulled*
- *½ cup (125ml) apple juice*
- *½ tsp. Gourmet Garden Mint*

Process all the ingredients in a blender until smooth.

Optional: Substitute Gourmet Garden Mint for 6 fresh mint leaves. Mint has a clean, fresh taste which is a welcome addition to all kinds of sweet and savoury dishes, as well as drinks and smoothies.

Marmalade

MAKES 3 CUPS

Inspired by Allison & Emma Robinson, Gayndah QLD.

- *2 oranges, roughly chopped, seeds removed*
- *2 grapefruits, roughly chopped, seeds removed*
- *2 tbs. Gourmet Garden Lemon Grass*
- *2¼ cups (495g) white sugar*

Place oranges and grapefruits in a deep, microwave safe dish and cover with water. Cook on high for 20 minutes or until the fruit is tender and transparent. Add sugar and stir well to combine. Cook for another 20–30 minutes, stirring every 5 minutes, until the marmalade starts to set. Stand for 5 minutes before pouring into clean, air-tight jars.

Tip: Place clean jars (without lids) in microwave and heat for 5–10 minutes or until hot. If jars have a metal seal, place the seal in a preheated 100°C oven for 5–10 minutes. It is important to have clean, sterilised jars in order for marmalade to keep well.

Parsley Omelette

MAKES 2

- 3 eggs
- 1 tsp. Gourmet Garden Parsley
- ½ cup (50g) grated cheese
- 1 tbs. (15g) butter

Beat whites of eggs stiffly with a pinch of salt. Lightly fold in yolks and 3 tbs. cold water, parsley then grated cheese. Melt butter in a pan and over medium heat pour in mixture. Cook till golden brown underneath. Brown top under griller or turn with egg flip and cook until golden.

Fact: Parsley is the world's most popular herb. It contains three times as much vitamin C as oranges, twice as much iron as spinach, is rich in vitamin A and contains folate, potassium and calcium.

Savoury Egg in a Hole

SERVES 2

- 2 tbs. (30g) butter
- 2 slices of bread
- 2 eggs
- 1 tsp. Gourmet Garden Chives

Melt butter and chives in a fry pan over low heat. Cut a 3cm hole from the centre of the bread slices and lay in the hot fry pan. When the side facing down is lightly toasted (about 2 minutes), flip and crack an egg into the hole of each slice of bread. Season with salt and pepper. Continue to cook until the egg is cooked and mostly firm. Flip again and cook for 1 minute. Serve immediately.

Tip: Ensure heat to melt butter and chives is low as chives cannot withstand high heat so are best added to a dish just before serving or as above.

Dips

*There is more hunger for love and appreciation
in this world than for bread.*

Mother Teresa

Avocado Cups

MAKES 8

Inspired by the beautiful Melinda Dines.

- *4 avocados*
- *½ Spanish onion, finely diced*
- *1 vine ripened tomato, diced*
- *1 tbs. Gourmet Garden Coriander*

Slice each avocado in half and remove the stone. Scrape 75% of the flesh into a bowl leaving the remaining cases intact. Roughly mash the flesh so that it is quite lumpy. Add the onion, tomato and coriander, season with sea salt and pepper. Mix well and fill the avocado cases with the mixture.

Optional: Serve with some lovely corn chips to dip ... Yummy!

Basil Pesto Dip

SERVES 4

- *1½ tbs. Gourmet Garden Basil*
- *2 tsp. Gourmet Garden Garlic*
- *75g parmesan cheese, grated*
- *¼ cup (60ml) extra virgin olive oil*

Blend all ingredients together and serve ... Easy and ultra tasty.

Corn Chips

SERVES 4

- *4 slices pita bread*
- *Extra virgin olive oil spray*
- *2 tbs. Gourmet Garden Garlic*

Preheat oven to 160°C. Cut pita bread into corn chip size pieces and spray with olive oil. Spread with garlic, season with sea salt and bake for 6–10 minutes or until crispy ... Serve with your favourite salsa or any of these fabulous dips.

Creamy Dill & Feta Spread

SERVES 4–6

- *230g cream cheese, softened*
- *230g crumbled feta cheese*
- *1 tsp. Gourmet Garden Garlic*
- *1 tbs. Gourmet Garden Dill*

In a medium bowl, thoroughly blend cream cheese, feta, garlic and dill with an electric mixer. Cover and refrigerate before serving.

Optional: This can be made ahead of time, the longer you leave it to rest prior to serving the longer the flavours have to infuse.

Fact: Dill helps to calm a nervous stomach and is known to kill intestinal bacteria.

Garlic Roasted Pepper Dip

SERVES 4–6

- *3 red peppers (capsicums), roasted and peeled*
- *125g cream cheese, softened*
- *1 tsp. Gourmet Garden Garlic*
- *½ cup fresh basil leaves, finely chopped*

Place first three ingredients along with sea salt and pepper into a blender and blend until smooth. Spoon mixture into a bowl, mix in half the basil leaves and stir to combine. Cover and refrigerate until set. Garnish with remaining basil leaves.

Tip: This dip is lovely made the day before to allow flavours time to develop. And if you have leftover basil consider using in tomato based dishes like soup and pasta sauces or add to egg and cheese dishes, sausage mixtures, salad dressings, salads, meat, chicken and fish. If you don't have fresh basil, substitute 1tbs. Gourmet Garden Basil.

Moroccan Hummus

SERVES 4

- *420g can chickpeas*
- *1 tsp. Gourmet Garden Moroccan Fresh Blend*
- *2 tbs. lemon juice*
- *1 tbs. tahini*

Drain the chickpeas, reserving the liquid. Blend all ingredients in a food processor adding a little liquid to reach desired consistency.

Optional: Serve with fresh vegetable sticks and crackers and substitute Gourmet Garden Garlic for Moroccan Fresh Blend to make an original hummus.

Pumpkin & Basil Dip

SERVES 4–6

A quick, easy and healthy dip.

- *330g pumpkin (butternut squash), peeled roughly and chopped into 3 cm cubes*
- *3 tsp. Gourmet Garden Garlic*
- *2 tsp. Gourmet Garden Basil*
- *½ cup (80g) cashews*

Toss pumpkin and garlic together and roast in a hot oven until soft. Allow to cool. Blend together pumpkin, basil and cashews and season to taste. Depending on consistency you may need to add a little water. Store in a refrigerator.

Rosemary Parmesan Biscuits

MAKES 36

These lovely treats are ideal served with afternoon drinks.

- *100g butter, chopped*
- *100g parmesan cheese, grated*
- *1 tsp. Gourmet Garden Rosemary*
- *¾ cup (130g) flour*

Place all ingredients in a blender, season and process until mixture forms a dough. Turn out onto a lightly floured surface, kneed and press into a 15cm disc. Wrap in greaseproof paper and refrigerate for 1 hour. Preheat oven to 180°C. Roll out the dough between two sheets of baking paper until ½ cm thick. Use a 5cm biscuit cutter to cut rounds from dough, repeating until all the dough is used. Place rounds onto paper lined baking trays and bake for 6–8 minutes or until lightly golden.

Tip: These yummy biscuits will keep for up to 4 days in a foil lined air-tight container.

Salmon Paté

SERVES 4

- *125g cream cheese, softened*
- *220g can pink salmon, drained*
- *1 tbs. lemon juice*
- *1 tbs. Gourmet Garden Dill*

Combine all and mix well.

Optional: Pile onto thick slices of Lebanese cucumber or serve with wedges of Lebanese bread.

Tapenade

MAKES 1 CUP

- *⅔ cup kalamata olives*
- *½ tsp. Gourmet Garden Garlic*
- *1 tbs. Gourmet Garden Basil*
- *1½ tbs. olive oil*

Place ingredients in a blender and process until smooth. Cover, chill and serve with crackers or Melba toast when needed.

Hint: Stir any leftover tapenade into pasta or spread onto warm toast with thinly sliced tomatoes and a slice of your favourite cheese.

Zucchini & Chive Dip

SERVES 4

- *200g cream cheese, softened*
- *3 tbs. milk*
- *1 cup shredded zucchini (courgette)*
- *1½ tbs. Gourmet Garden Chives*

In a bowl, mix cream cheese and milk until well blended. Mix in the zucchini, chives and a good pinch of salt. Chill in refrigerator for 1 hour before serving.

Tip: Chives are considered one of the "fine herbs" of French cuisine, and great to boost the flavour of salads, soups, sandwiches, dips, dressings and sour cream.

Condiments

*Condiments have been used to enhance the flavour of foods
since ancient times. The first condiment was salt, vinegar followed.
Pesto sauce was invented in the 16th century in Italy.
A French Chef first made mayonnaise in 1756 and Ketchup
began its life as a Chinese fish sauce called Ke-tsiap.*

Aioli

MAKES ½ CUP

- *½ cup (130g) whole egg mayonnaise*
- *½ tsp. Gourmet Garden Garlic*
- *2 tsp. lemon juice*
- *2 tsp. Dijon mustard*

Mix all together, season with sea salt and pepper and chill for several hours before serving, allowing time for flavours to infuse.

Optional: Add 1 tsp. honey if you have it. Delicious served with all types of seafood, wedges and thick cut chips. Enjoy!

Asian Dipping Sauce

MAKES ½ CUP

Serve with any meat and Asian steamed vegetables.

- *½ tsp. Gourmet Garden Garlic*
- *¼ cup (60ml) sweet chilli sauce*
- *¼ cup (60ml) soy sauce*
- *1 tsp. Gourmet Garden Ginger*

Combine all ingredients and mix well.

Tip: Gourmet Garden Ginger combines well with soy sauce to marinate fish or stir through steamed carrots.

Balsamic & Garlic Dressing

MAKES 1 CUP

- *2 tbs. balsamic vinegar*
- *¼ cup (60ml) lemon juice*
- *½ tsp. Gourmet Garden Garlic*
- *¾ cup (185ml) olive oil*

Combine all ingredients in a screw top jar and shake well.

Tip: If you have lemons remaining, a fabulous way to start any day is with a glass of lemon water. Both lemons and water help flush out toxins in your system. Although lemons are acidic, they are alkalizing in your body.

Chilli Dipping Sauce

MAKES ¼ CUP

- *2 tbs. sugar*
- *1 tsp. Gourmet Garden Garlic*
- *1 tsp. Gourmet Garden Chilli*
- *2 tsp. fish sauce*

Boil sugar with ½ cup (125ml) water, gourmet herbs and fish sauce until reduced by half. Great in stir-fries, salads or as a dipping sauce for BBQ chicken wings.

Hint: You can control how hot you like your chilli by selecting either Gourmet Garden Hot or Mild Chilli varieties.

Dill Yoghurt Dressing

MAKES APPROX. ½ CUP

- *150g natural yoghurt*
- *1 tsp. Gourmet Garden Dill*
- *½ tsp. Gourmet Garden Garlic*
- *1 tsp. fresh lemon juice*

Combine all ingredients in a bowl and mix well.

Optional: This is super delish served over baked beetroot wedges (See: Vegetables) or drizzled over your favourite piece of grilled fish or salmon.

Herbal Fruit Salad Dressing

MAKES ¼ CUP

This is sensational.

- *2 tbs. Gourmet Garden Mint*
- *2 tbs. Gourmet Garden Ginger*
- *2 tsp. fresh lemon juice*
- *2 tsp. honey*

Simply mix together and toss through a freshly cut fruit salad. This provides a delicious way to start the day drizzled over your favourite fruit salad.

Mango & Coriander Salsa

SERVES 4–6

- *1 lime*
- *½ red finger chilli*
- *1 mango, cubed*
- *1–2 tbs. Gourmet Garden Coriander*

Cut the lime in half, juice and zest one half. Cut chilli in half, remove the seeds and chop very finely. Gently toss all ingredients to combine, adding sea salt and pepper to taste. Serve with grilled fish or prawns.

Optional: Substitute red finger chilli for 1 tsp. Gourmet Garden Chilli.

Tip: Coriander blends especially well with both chilli and garlic.

Mint Sauce

MAKES APPROX. ½ CUP

This is a lovely glaze served over roast lamb.

- *1 tsp. Gourmet Garden Mint*
- *2 tbs. lemon juice*
- *1 tbs. sugar*

Place all ingredients plus 4 tbs. boiling water into a small saucepan and simmer over a low heat for 5 minutes. Allow to stand for 30 minutes before serving.

Optional: Another fabulous variation to this is to place fresh or dried mint leaves in a small heatproof jug, add sugar to taste and a little boiling water. Stir, cover and let stand for about 30 minutes and then add malt vinegar to taste, stir and serve with lamb.

Parsley & Lemon Salad Dressing

MAKES ¼ CUP

- 2 tbs. olive oil
- 2 tbs. lemon juice
- 2 tsp. brown sugar
- 1 tsp. Gourmet Garden Parsley

Simply combine all ingredients together in a screw top jar and shake. Serve drizzled over a lovely fresh salad and enjoy.

Fact: Parsley has very high levels of vitamin C and helps strengthen the digestive system. It is the world's most popular herb.

Parsley Vinaigrette

MAKES 1 CUP

- ½ cup (125ml) olive oil
- ½ cup (125ml) white wine vinegar
- 1 tbs. Gourmet Garden Parsley
- 2 tsp. Dijon mustard

Combine all ingredients in a screw-top jar and shake well.

Fact: Apart from adding flavour, mustards also help stimulate the appetite. Mustards are made from the dried powdered seeds of white or black mustard mixed with water, wine or vinegar.

Peanut, Chilli, Coriander & Lime Salsa

MAKES APPROX. 1 CUP

This is just amazing served over almost anything!

- *½ cup (60g) coarsely chopped, roasted peanuts*
- *1 tbs. Gourmet Garden Coriander*
- *1 tbs. sweet chilli sauce*
- *1 tbs. lime juice and a sprinkling of zest*

Combine all ingredients in a small bowl and toss gently.

Red Wine & Garlic Gravy

SERVES 6

- *1 pkt dry gravy mix*
- *½ tsp. Gourmet Garden Garlic*
- *½ cup (125ml) red wine*
- *½ cup (125ml) cold water*

In a small saucepan, mix together all the ingredients and bring to the boil over medium heat. Stir for about 1 minute or until thickened.

Satay Sauce

MAKES 1 CUP

- ½ cup (110g) crunchy peanut butter
- 2 tbs. sweet chilli sauce
- ¾ cup (185g) liquid vegetable stock
- 1 tbs. Gourmet Garden Coriander

Combine peanut butter, sweet chilli sauce and stock and cook stirring continually for 2–3 minutes. Swirl through coriander.

Optional: Delicious served with wedges and a selection of freshly cut vegetables (cucumber, carrot, celery, cherry tomatoes, mushrooms etc).

Thai Dressing

MAKES ¼ CUP

Y.U.M.M.Y!

- 1 tbs. Gourmet Garden Thai Fresh Blend
- 1 tbs. fish sauce
- 1 tbs. brown sugar or palm sugar
- 1 lime, juiced

Pop all ingredients into a jar, seal and shake well to combine.

Optional: This is SCRUMPTIOUS tossed through a fresh Asian salad with glass noodles and topped with either thinly sliced beef, grilled chicken or cooked prawns (shrimp).

Cocktail Food

Gourmet Garden leads the industry in natural flavour development and produces the world's most flavoursome and aromatic pre-prepared herbs and spices.

Fresh Made Easy™

Brie & Quince Matchsticks

MAKES 4

- *1 sheet ready rolled puff pastry, cut into six lengths*
- *2 tbs. Gourmet Garden Lemon Grass*
- *2 tbs. quince paste*
- *250g brie cheese*

Preheat oven to 200°C. Place pastry on a paper lined baking tray and blind bake for 8–10 minutes. Remove and spread immediately with lemon grass and quince and then slices of brie.

Tip: Blind baking, sometimes called pre-baking, is the process of baking a pie crust or other pastry without the filling or topping. It is necessary when the filling has a shorter bake time than the crust and it also helps prevent the pie crust from becoming soggy from its filling.

Brie Bruschetta

SERVES 4–6

- *1 crusty French stick, sliced 2–3cm thick*
- *6–8 ripe tomatoes, chopped*
- *2 tbs. Gourmet Garden Basil*
- *250g brie cheese*

Under grill, toast one side of each French stick slice. Remove and turn over. Brush un-toasted side with basil and some of the juices that result when you chop the tomatoes. Lay a slice of brie on each slice and grill for a further 2–3 minutes or until cheese has melted. Top with chopped tomatoes and season with sea salt and pepper.

BBQ Garlic Prawns

MAKES 24

- *1 tsp. Gourmet Garden Garlic*
- *1 tsp. Gourmet Garden Coriander*
- *3 lemons (grated zest of one)*
- *24 large green prawns (shrimp), peeled, deveined with tails in place*

Combine garlic, coriander, lemon juice and rind of 1 lemon in a large bowl and season to taste. Add prawns and toss to coat well. Cover and refrigerate, marinating for 1 hour. Drain prawns, reserving marinade, and thread onto skewers. Cook prawns for 2–3 minutes each side brushing with marinade until pink and cooked through. Cut remaining 2 lemons in half and, cut side down, cook for 1–2 minutes or until glazed. Serve with crusty bread to soak up the juices.

Fact: Garlic is extremely versatile and is found in many stir-fries, pastas and curries. From pizza to poultry, garlic truly is one of the world's natural wonders!

Cheese & Coriander Quesadillas

SERVES 2

- *4 small tortillas*
- *½ cup (85g) salsa*
- *⅔ cup shredded cheddar cheese*
- *2 tsp. Gourmet Garden Coriander*

Place 2 tortillas on a baking tray lined with baking paper. Mix together the salsa and coriander. Top each with salsa, cheese and remaining tortillas. Cook in a fry pan for 4 minutes each side or until golden brown.

Fact: One of the oldest herbs known to man and originating in the Mediterranean, coriander's bold, lingering flavour is often used in curries, soups and stir-fries. Coriander is also ideal for adding flavour in sauces, salads and vegetable dishes.

Chorizo with Parsley & Olives

SERVES 6

- *650g chorizo sausage, cut into rounds*
- *1 tsp. Gourmet Garden Parsley*
- *85g black olives*

Heat a large fry pan and cook sausage turning frequently over medium heat for 4 minutes. Add parsley and olives and cook, stirring constantly, for 3 minutes or until heated. Serve immediately using toothpicks ... Yummy!

Fact: Chorizo sausages are made from pork that has been generously flavoured with garlic, onion, chilli, oregano and cumin. Although recipes do vary, they are an important ingredient in Paella and also add a boost to casseroles and soups.

Green Eyed Pickles

SERVES 4–6

A recipe by the delightful Marie McColl.

These are fast, fresh and fun!

- *4 green pickles (cucumbers, gherkins, dill pickles)*
- *4 slices sandwich ham*
- *125g cream cheese, softened*
- *1 tbs. Gourmet Garden Italian Herbs*

Dry pickles. Lay the ham onto a clean, flat surface and spread evenly with the cream cheese and Italian herbs. Place pickles down the centre of the ham, season lightly before rolling tight. Chill before slicing into circles to serve.

Marinated & Baked Olives

SERVES 6

- *500g mixed olives, pitted*
- *1 lemon*
- *2 sprigs rosemary, leaves chopped*
- *2 tsp. Gourmet Garden Garlic*

Preheat oven to 200°C. Place olives in a baking dish and with a rolling pin, gently push down so skin splits. Onto the olives, grate the zest of a lemon, then toss through rosemary and garlic. Cook for 15 minutes and serve warm.

Optional: If fresh rosemary is unavailable substitute 1 tbs. Gourmet Garden Rosemary.

Minted Lamb Balls

SERVES 4

A recipe from Janelle McCosker.

- *500g minced lamb*
- *½ an onion, finely diced*
- *1 tsp. curry powder*
- *1 tbs. Gourmet Garden Mint*

Mix all ingredients together and roll into bite-sized balls and fry in a non-stick pan until crunchy on the outside (this means they are cooked well on the inside).

Optional: These are lovely served with Aioli (see: Condiments).

Oysters with Mango Chilli

MAKES 12

- *12 oysters on the half shell*
- *1 tsp. lime juice*
- *1 tsp. Gourmet Garden Chilli*
- *½ firm mango, chopped finely*

Place oysters in a single layer on serving platter. Mix mango, chilli and lime juice together and divide among oysters.

Prosciutto Wrapped Haloumi

SERVES 6

- *500g punnets cherry tomatoes*
- *300g haloumi (cut into 6 x 1cm thick slices)*
- *6 slices prosciutto*
- *1 tbs. Gourmet Garden Basil*

Preheat oven to 200°C. Cut tomatoes in half and place into a bowl. Gently mix through basil then place onto a paper lined baking tray. Bake for 15 minutes or until soft. Wrap haloumi slices with prosciutto. Heat a non-stick fry pan over medium heat and cook haloumi in batches on both sides until browned. Arrange haloumi on plates and top with tomatoes and their juices.

Optional: This is a fabulous starter and lovely served with grissini.

Salmon Blinis

SERVES 6

- *150g pkt. blinis*
- *1 pkt smoked salmon*
- *1 tub crème fraîche*
- *2 tsp. Gourmet Garden Dill*

Top blinis with smoked salmon and a dollop of crème fraîche mixed with dill.

Optional: Pita breads work just as well as blinis.

Thai Chicken Balls

SERVES 8

These are just soooo gooood!

- *500g chicken mince*
- *1 spring onion, finely diced*
- *2 tbs. Gourmet Garden Thai Fresh Blend*
- *1 tbs. Gourmet Garden Coriander*

Mix all ingredients together and then using a tablespoon roll into balls and in a non-stick fry pan, on a medium-high heat, cook for 6 minutes or until browned and cooked through.

Optional: Serve with a little sweet chilli sauce to dip.

Morning & Afternoon Teas

Everyone knows of the marriage made in heaven which is that of chocolate and mint. Perhaps this is why the recent trend of adding herbs to sweets makes for a number of exciting recipes.

Almond & Ginger Stuffed Dates

MAKES 24

- *100g blanched almonds*
- *24 (about 400g) fresh dates*
- *1 tsp. Gourmet Garden Ginger*

Preheat oven to 180°C. Scatter the almonds over a baking tray and bake for 6 minutes or until toasted. Whilst cooling, use a small, sharp knife to cut a slit in each date. Remove stones, place a small amount of ginger and stand 2–3 toasted almonds in each date cavity. Arrange on a serving plate.

Tip: Toasting the almonds first releases their flavour and makes for a delicious treat in this recipe.

Chocolate Chilli Lychees

SERVES 6

These are elegant, easy & amazing served anytime.

- *200g dark chocolate*
- *1 tsp. Gourmet Garden Chilli*
- *400g tin lychees, drained and dried*

Add the chocolate and chilli to a double boiler and gently melt. Dip lychees, coating well, place on a paper lined tray and set in fridge.

Chocolate Stacks

MAKES 25

- *250g dark chocolate*
- *200g slivered almonds, halved and lightly toasted*
- *½ cup (185g) sultanas*
- *1 tbs. Gourmet Garden Ginger*

Melt chocolate in microwave. Remove from heat as soon as completely melted. Add remaining ingredients to the chocolate and mix well. Spoon small amounts 2cm apart on a paper lined baking tray. Refrigerate until hardened then serve. Store parcels in an airtight container and refrigerate.

Coconut & Mint Balls

MAKES 40

Everyone loooves these.

- *4 cups (480g) desiccated coconut*
- *400g can condensed milk*
- *Zest of 1 lemon*
- *2 tbs. Gourmet Garden Mint*

Preheat oven to 180°C. Place all ingredients in a bowl and mix to combine. Using a tsp. roll mixture into balls and place on two paper lined baking trays. Bake for 12 minutes or until the balls are lightly browned. Remove and cool before serving.

Date & Ginger Loaf

Absolutely heavenly!

- *375g pkt dates, chopped*
- *2 tsp. instant coffee*
- *1 tbs. Gourmet Garden Ginger*
- *1 cup (175g) self raising flour*

Add coffee to 1 cup (250ml) of boiling water and mix. Pour over dates and soak overnight. Stir in flour. Pour mixture into a paper lined loaf tin and bake in a preheated 160°C oven for 45 minutes.

Optional: Serve warm with lashings of butter.

Ginger Macaroons

MAKES 20

- *1 egg white*
- *½ cup (100g) caster sugar*
- *1 cup (170g) almond meal*
- *1 tsp. Gourmet Garden Ginger*

Preheat oven to 180°C. Whisk egg white until stiff peaks form, gradually adding sugar until a thick, white consistency. Fold in almond meal and ginger. Place spoonfuls of the mixture on paper lined baking trays, allowing space for spreading. Bake for 20 minutes or until golden and just turning crisp.

Fruit Cake

SERVES 10

Absolutely Delicious!

- *1 kg mixed fruit*
- *800g can mango in syrup*
- *2 tbs. Gourmet Garden Ginger*
- *2 cups (350g) self raising flour*

Soak mixed fruit in mango pieces and syrup with a ¼ cup (60ml) of water overnight. Stir flour into soaked fruit and mix well. Spoon mixture into a 22cm lined cake tin. Bake for 2–2½ hours in the bottom of a preheated 125°C oven or until cooked through. Remove and leave to cool. Place in an air tight container or wrap in foil.

Optional: Add a shot of your favourite tipple, sherry, brandy, rum, grand marnier.

Fruit Mint Palmiers

- *2 tbs. caster sugar*
- *1 sheet ready rolled puff pastry*
- *110g fruit mince*
- *1 tbs. Gourmet Garden Mint*

Preheat oven to 200°C. Line a baking tray with baking paper and sprinkle sugar onto it. Lay pastry on the paper and spread the entire surface with mince and mint. Roll up one side tightly until you reach the middle then repeat with the other side. Freeze for 30 minutes before removing and slicing into 1cm thick slices. Bake for 15–20 minutes or until golden brown.

Fruit Slice

SERVES 8

- 400g can condensed milk
- 375g mixed fruit
- 1 cup (175g) self raising flour
- 1 tsp. Gourmet Garden Rosemary

Preheat oven to 160°C. Mix all ingredients together and pour into a baking paper lined baking dish. Bake for 40–45 minutes or until cooked when tested. Allow to cool and slice. Can be kept in freezer for up to one month.

Optional: For a flavour variation add one cup of coconut to the mixture before baking. This is lovely served topped with lemon icing (see: 4 Ingredients 2).

Fact: Gourmet Garden Rosemary is grown without the use of artificial pesticides, herbicides or fertilisers.

Jam Tarts

MAKES 12

- 1 sheet short crust pastry
- ⅔ cup (200g) strawberry jam
- 2 tbs. Gourmet Garden Lemon Grass
- ½ cup cream, whipped

Lay pastry flat and cut as many circles as possible, press each circle into a lightly buttered patty cake tin, pressing a fork down around the edges for decoration. Cook at 180°C for around 8–10 minutes. Mix jam and lemon grass together and spoon the desired amount into each shell, return to the oven for another 5 minutes. Allow to cool and set before topping with a dollop of freshly whipped cream.

Rosemary Shortbread

MAKES 12

- 1½ cups unsalted butter
- ⅔ cup (135g) caster sugar
- 2¾ cups (480g) plain flour
- 1 tsp. Gourmet Garden Rosemary

In a medium bowl, cream together the butter and sugar until light and fluffy. Stir in the flour, ¼ tsp. salt and rosemary until well blended. The dough will be somewhat soft. Cover and refrigerate for 1 hour. Preheat oven to 190°C. Line a baking tray with baking paper. On a lightly floured surface, roll the dough out in a large round circle about 1cm thickness. Cut into triangle wedges, without cutting all the way through. Prick the top with a fork and sprinkle with remaining sugar. Bake for 8 minutes in oven or until golden at the edges. Cool before breaking each wedge. Store in an airtight container at room temperature.

White Choc Chilli Macadamias

SERVES 4

- 150g white chocolate
- 1 tbs. Gourmet Garden Chilli, brought to room temperature
- 100g whole macadamia nuts, toasted

Melt chocolate carefully in a bowl in the microwave, stirring every 15 seconds. Cool slightly then add chilli and stir until combined. Add macadamia nuts in batches and coat well. Place on a paper lined baking tray and chill prior to serving.

Light Meals & Lunches

Over 4 centuries ago, Leonardo da Vinci said,

*"May we ever have joy and gratitude in our hearts that
the creator of all things, in his love for us, placed the herbs
in the fields for our healing."*

Beef & Basil Baguette

SERVES 2

- *¼ cup (65g) mayonnaise*
- *1 tbs. Gourmet Garden Basil*
- *½ a fresh baguette*
- *2 thick slices of roast beef*

Mix together mayonnaise and basil. Cut baguette in half and spread
on mayo mix. Top with roast beef. Add any other sandwich filling such
as lettuce and tomato if desired.

Chorizo & Potato Frittata

SERVES 4

- *800g Desiree potatoes, peeled and cut into 2cm pieces*
- *3 chorizo sausages*
- *7 eggs*
- *2 tbs. Gourmet Garden Parsley*

Par cook potatoes in microwave for 4–6 minutes. Heat a non-stick fry pan with a heat resistant handle then add chorizo and cook for 3 minutes or until golden, remove. Using the juices from the sausage add potatoes and cook for 8–10 minutes or until they start to crisp. Reduce heat to medium/low and return chorizo to pan. Beat eggs and parsley and season. Pour over potato mixture and give a little shake. Over a low heat, cook for 10 minutes before removing to place under the grill for 5 minutes or until firm and golden. Cut into wedges and serve.

Chilli Chicken Wings

SERVES 4

- *500g chicken wings*
- *1 lime, juiced*
- *1 tbs. Gourmet Garden Garlic*
- *2 tbs. Gourmet Garden Chilli*

Preheat oven to 200°C. Remove tips from wings and cut in 2 at the elbow. Arrange in a single layer on baking tray lined with baking paper. Cook for 20 minutes or until almost done. Meanwhile combine lime juice, garlic and chilli. Remove wings from oven and baste both sides with mixture. Return to oven and cook for a further 5 minutes. Remove, baste and return to cook for a final 5 minutes.

Optional: Serve garnished with lime zest or wedges.

Ham and Egg Quiches

MAKES 6

- 6 ham off the bone round slices
- 6 eggs
- 1 tbs. Gourmet Garden Parsley
- 1 cup grated cheese

Preheat oven to 180°C. Line 6 large non-stick muffin cases with ham. Beat eggs, add parsley and season with sea salt and pepper. Mix before pouring into ham lined muffin cases. Sprinkle evenly with cheese. Bake for 20 minutes or until set.

Lemon Grass & Chicken Soup

SERVES 4

An easy soup packed with flavour and texture.

- 1ltr. chicken stock
- 4 sliced chicken thigh fillets
- 300g can of creamed corn
- 2 tbs. Gourmet Garden Lemon Grass

Bring chicken stock to the boil. Add chicken thigh fillets and creamed corn. Simmer for 15 minutes. Stir through Lemon Grass. Simmer for another 5 minutes, season to taste then serve.

Pumpkin, Ginger & Garlic Soup

SERVES 4–6

- *1 butternut pumpkin (butternut squash), diced*
- *1 ltr. chicken stock*
- *1 tbs. Gourmet Garden Garlic*
- *2 tbs. Gourmet Garden Ginger*

Place all ingredients into a saucepan and cover with water. Bring to the boil, then reduce heat and simmer for approx. 15 minutes or until soft and tender. Blend until smooth.

Optional: Serve with a swirl of cream.

Roasted Tomato & Basil Soup

SERVES 4

- *12 Roma tomatoes, chopped*
- *2 red onions, chopped*
- *5 tbs. tomato paste*
- *3 tbs. Gourmet Garden Basil*

Preheat oven to 200°C. Place tomatoes and onions on a baking tray in the oven coated with tomato paste. Cook for 30 minutes. Place in a food processor and blend. Stir in basil. Add salted water to reduce thickness. Season with cracked black pepper.

Sausage Rolls

SERVES 4

Y.U.M.M.Y Y.U.M.M.Y

- *500g lean mince*
- *1 carrot, peeled and grated*
- *1 tbs. Gourmet Garden Coriander*
- *2 sheets ready rolled puff pastry*

Preheat oven 180°C. Place first three ingredients into a bowl and mix well. Season with sea salt and pepper. Cut the pastry sheets in half and dollop spoonfuls down the centre of each slice. Brush the sides of pastry with water and roll up. Cut into desired thickness, place on a lined baking tray, seam side down, and mark tops with a knife. Bake for 15–20 minutes.

Optional: Add a quarter a cup of sultanas to the mix if you have them. Baste pastry with milk prior to baking for a golden finish.

Spicy BBQ Calamari

SERVES 4

- *Juice of 1 lemon*
- *1 tbs. Gourmet Garden Coriander*
- *1 tsp. Gourmet Garden Chilli*
- *4 calamari tubes, scored and cut into strips*

Combine lemon juice, coriander, chilli and cracked pepper in a bowl. Coat calamari in mixture and refrigerate for 1 hour. Cook on a very hot BBQ until brown. Serve with lemon wedges and a fresh simple salad.

Summer Thai BBQ Prawns

SERVES 4

- ½ lime, juiced
- 2 tbs. olive oil
- 2 tbs. Gourmet Garden Thai Fresh Blend
- 500g peeled and deveined prawns (shrimp)

Combine lime juice, 1 tbs. olive oil and Thai blend into a bowl and mix well. On a very hot BBQ plate add 1 tbs. of olive oil and then the prawns. Drizzle ¾ of mixture over prawns and cook until brown and tender. Serve prawns drizzled with remaining mixture and lime wedges.

Thai Beef Koftas

MAKES 16

- 1 tbs. crunchy peanut butter
- 2 tbs. Gourmet Garden Thai Fresh Blend
- 1 egg
- 500g lean beef mince

Warm peanut butter in a microwave on high for 30 seconds to soften. Mix in Thai Blend and egg. Add to mince and combine. Roll mixture into fat sausage shapes, insert a damp skewer and grill or BBQ until cooked.

Optional: Roll into patties and serve as a burger or in pitta bread with fresh green salad … Mmmmm!

Toasted French Bread

SERVES 6

- *1 long French baguette*
- *125g butter, softened*
- *¾ cup parmesan cheese*
- *2 tsp. Gourmet Garden Mild Chilli*

Preheat ovento 150°C. Slice bread in half lengthways, then thirds. Combine all other ingredients, season and mix well. Spread over the slices of bread and bake for 15 minutes or until heated through and golden on top. Slice and serve warm with any soup.

Optional: Substitute Chilli for Gourmet Garden Garlic.

Zucchini, Leek & Mint Soup

SERVES 4

- *1 zucchini (courgette), grated*
- *1 leek, peeled and finely chopped*
- *1 tbs. Gourmet Garden Mint*
- *3 cups (750ml) chicken stock*

Place all ingredients in a medium saucepan. Bring to the boil, reduce heat and simmer for 20 minutes. Season and serve.

Tip: For a long, happy 'leek' life ... Trim and discard the top, keep in a plastic bag in the crisper section of your refrigerator for up to 1 week.

Sides

*In the 1930's, Californian produce visionary Bruce Church,
started packing and shipping fresh heads of lettuce across the USA in
ice-packed rail cars. It was then that the popular name 'iceberg' lettuce
was born. As the trains trundled by many a shout could be heard
"The icebergs are coming, the icebergs are coming!"*

Salads

Asparagus with Thai Dressing

SERVES 6–8

A light and lovely Asian inspired dish.

- *2 bunches of fresh asparagus*
- *1 tbs. lime juice*
- *2 tsp. Gourmet Garden Thai Fresh Blend*
- *8 iceberg lettuce leaves*

Trim each asparagus stem of its woody end. Steam or grill for
3–4 minutes or until just tender. Meanwhile mix lime juice, a little zest
and Thai herbs. Arrange crisp lettuce leaves on a long white platter,
top with asparagus and drizzle with yummy dressing.

*Tip: Tender green asparagus tips are delicious in omelettes, quiches
or served as part of a salad. They can also be stir-fried until tender
and crisp. A high heat quickly cooks the vegetables and retains
maximum flavour.*

Carrot & Walnut Salad

SERVES 4

- 4 carrots, peeled and grated
- ½ tbs. Gourmet Garden Garlic
- ½ cup (50g) walnuts, chopped
- 4 tbs. whole egg mayonnaise

Mix all ingredients together and serve.

Optional: Substitute carrots for beetroots.

Curried Eggs

MAKES 12

- 6 hardboiled eggs
- 2 tbs. egg mayonnaise
- ½ tsp. curry powder
- ½ tsp. Gourmet Garden Parsley

Peel eggs and cut in half lengthwise. Remove yolks and mash. Add mayonnaise, curry powder, parsley and season with sea salt and pepper. Place (or pipe) yolk mixture back into the egg halves.

Optional: Substitute salad cream for mayonnaise.

Garden Salad

SERVES 6

- 150g mixed salad leaves
- 100g cherry tomatoes, halved
- ¼ cup (60ml) balsamic vinegar
- ½ tsp. Gourmet Garden Oregano

Place salad leaves and tomatoes in a large bowl. Season with sea salt and pepper, then toss with balsamic vinegar mixed with oregano. Once dressed, serve immediately.

Optional: This is also nice served with thickly diced avocados.

Pea & Feta Salad

SERVES 4

- 2 cups fresh peas
- 1 tbs. Gourmet Garden Mint
- 1 cup feta cheese, crumbled
- 2 tbs. fresh lemon juice

Place peas in a serving dish and allow to sit in boiling water for 2–3 minutes. Drain and rinse under cold water, allow to dry. Add mint and feta. Drizzle with juice and toss gently to combine.

Hint: Feta cheese is traditionally made from ewe's or goat's milk. It keeps well if stored in a screw-top jar or polythene wrapper in the fridge.

Potato Salad

SERVES 4–6

- 4 potatoes, washed and cubed
- 4 rashers of bacon, chopped and fried until crisp
- 1 tbs. Gourmet Garden Mint
- ¼ cup (60ml) whole egg mayonnaise

Boil potatoes until tender, approx. 6–8 minutes and completely cool. Toss with remaining ingredients. Season if desired. Keep chilled prior to serving.

Tomato & Bocconcini Salad

SERVES 4

- 4 vine-ripened tomatoes, sliced
- 2 tbs. extra virgin olive oil
- 1 tbs. Gourmet Garden Basil
- 4 bocconcini (buffalo mozzarella), thinly sliced

Arrange tomato slices on a large flat serving plate. Mix together oil and basil and drizzle over tomatoes. Top with slices of bocconcini. Season generously with sea salt and pepper, cover and chill before serving.

Warm Mediterranean Salad

SERVES 4

Recipe by Kate Madden.

- *16 cherry tomatoes, halved*
- *⅓ cup (50g) pine nuts*
- *1 tbs. Gourmet Garden Garlic*
- *120g pkt baby spinach*

Heat a wok on high and toss in tomatoes and pine nuts, stir in garlic for 1 minute before adding spinach. Gently toss for 30 seconds, remove from heat and serve with BBQ or grilled meat or on its own.

Potato

Did you know: The Potato is the most important
non-cereal crop in the world and fourth overall?
Only corn, wheat and rice are more important.

Basil Baked Potatoes

SERVES 4

- *3 medium potatoes, peeled and thinly sliced*
- *1 medium onion, thinly sliced*
- *1 tbs. Gourmet Garden Basil*
- *4 tbs. (60g) butter, melted*

Preheat oven to 180°C. Place half the sliced potatoes and half the sliced onions in a buttered 22cm pie dish. Mix together the butter and basil and drizzle over potatoes. Repeat layers of potatoes ending with remaining melted butter. Season with sea salt and pepper and cover with foil. Bake for 20 minutes, uncover and bake for 15–20 minutes longer or until potatoes are tender.

Double Baked Chive Potatoes

SERVES 4

- *4 potatoes, washed*
- *½ cup (160g) sour cream*
- *2 tbs. Gourmet Garden Chives*

Preheat oven to 200°C. With a sharp knife, pierce each potato 2–3 times before wrapping in foil. Place on a baking tray and bake for 1 hour or until tender when pierced with a fork. Remove and allow to cool, cut the top off each potato and remove the cooked flesh, leaving the skin intact. Mash the potato with sour cream and chives. Pile the mixture back into the potato skins. Add lid and return to the oven and bake for a further 10 minutes.

Optional: As a general rule, a typical 300g potato should be baked for approx. 1 hour.

Garlic Mash

SERVES 4–6

- *2½ cups (625ml) chicken stock*
- *5 large potatoes, peeled and cubed*
- *2 heaped tsp. Gourmet Garden Garlic*
- *1 tbs. (15g) butter*

Place stock and potatoes in a large saucepan and bring to the boil. Cook for 20 minutes or until tender. Drain potatoes, reserving the stock. Mash the potatoes, garlic and butter together and slowly add stock to give desired consistency. Beat in a generous dash of black pepper.

Fact: Gourmet Garden Garlic is now certified organic and grown without the use of artificial pesticides, herbicides or fertilisers.

Hot Chilli Mash

SERVES 4–6

For a different twist on mashed potatoes.

- *800g potatoes, peeled and cubed*
- *1 tbs. (15g) butter*
- *¼ cup (60ml) milk*
- *1 tsp. Gourmet Garden Chilli*

Boil potatoes for about 15–20 minutes or until cooked through. Drain and add milk and butter and mash until fluffy. Stir in chilli and serve immediately.

Optional: Lovely served with any meat, chicken or fish dish and a side of steamed greens.

Mashed Sweet Potatoes

SERVES 6

- *1 kg sweet potatoes, peeled and chopped*
- *3 tbs. maple syrup*
- *½ tsp. Gourmet Garden Ginger*
- *⅛ tsp. ground cinnamon*

Pop potatoes in a microwave safe dish and microwave on high for approx. 4–6 minutes or until tender. Drain, and mash with syrup and spices.

Optional: Top with toasted flaked almonds if desired.

Potato Bake

SERVES 4

- 4 large potatoes, peeled and cut into 1cm slices
- 1½ cups grated mozzarella cheese (reserve ½ cup)
- 1 tbs. Gourmet Garden Garlic
- 250ml sour cream

Preheat oven to 180°C. Lightly steam potatoes for 15 minutes, or until just soft, set aside. Combine cheese, garlic and sour cream in a bowl. Line the base of a baking dish with the steamed potato. Alternate a layer of potatoes with liquid. Top with reserved cheese and bake for 30–40 minutes or until tender.

Roasted Potatoes with Lemon & Garlic

SERVES 4

- 2 tbs. lemon juice
- 1 tbs. olive oil
- 2 tsp. Gourmet Garden Garlic
- 600g potatoes, peeled and cut into 2–3cm cubes

Preheat oven to 220°C. Combine lemon juice, olive oil and garlic along with a pinch of salt in a bowl. Toss in potatoes and let stand for 10 minutes. Spoon mixture into a baking dish and bake for 45–50 minutes or until tender and lightly browned, stir occasionally.

Rosemary & Thyme Roasted Potatoes

SERVES 4

These are lovely served with almost anything!

- *4 large potatoes*
- *2 tbs. olive oil*
- *1 tbs. Gourmet Garden Rosemary*
- *1 tbs. fresh thyme leaves*

Preheat oven to 180°C. Peel potatoes and halve. On the non-flat side, make 4 or 5 slices across the potatoes, slicing about three-quarters of the way through. Combine potatoes with oil in large baking dish, sprinkle with sea salt and pepper. Bake for 20 minutes, remove, coat with rosemary and sprinkle with thyme. Bake for a further 10 minutes or until potatoes are golden and tender.

Tip: Rosemary adds flavour to many roasted vegetables, marinades, meat and salads. These are also delicious substituting rosemary and thyme for Gourmet Garden Italian Herbs.

Sweet Potato & Beetroot Wedges

SERVES 6–8

- 600g sweet potato, peeled and cut into wedges
- 3 beetroots, unpeeled and cut into wedges
- ¼ cup (125ml) olive oil
- 2 tbs. Gourmet Garden Lemon Grass

Preheat oven to 200°C. Place the prepared vegetables in a baking dish. Mix together oil and lemon grass, pour over the vegetables and mix to evenly coat. Bake for 25–35 minutes or until tender and golden brown.

Optional: These are fabulous served with Dill Yoghurt Dressing (See: Condiments).

Wedges with Garlic & Rosemary

SERVES 6–8

- 6–8 potatoes, peeled and cut into wedges
- 4 tbs. olive oil
- 1 tsp. Gourmet Garden Garlic
- 1 tbs. Gourmet Garden Rosemary

Preheat oven to 200°C. Simply mix together olive oil, garlic and rosemary. Coat wedges in mixture and roast for 20 minutes or until golden brown. Sprinkle with a little sea salt and serve.

Optional: Substitute rosemary with oregano and serve with sour cream.

Fact: In 1995 potato plants were taken into space on the Space Shuttle 'Columbia', this marked the first time any food was ever grown in space.

Vegetables

Vegetables are NUTRIENT DENSE ... One of the healthiest eating habits you can foster in your family is to make vegetables the centrepiece of your meals and let the other food groups accompany them. For many families this may be a switch of mindset from meat and potatoes to potatoes and meat, but there are so many fresh, delicious vegetables available today it's never been easier.

BBQ Corn with Italian Herbs

MAKES 4

- 4 corn cobs
- 4 tsp. (30g) butter
- 4 tsp. Gourmet Garden Italian Herbs

Remove husks from each corn cob and place in foil. Top each with 1 tsp. Italian Herbs and 1 tsp. butter. Seal parcel. BBQ for 15–20 minutes and serve as an accompaniment to your meal.

Tip: Add Gourmet Garden Italian Herbs to your favourite spaghetti bolognaise recipe for that authentic Mediterranean flavour.

Caramelized Zucchini with Mint

SERVES 4

- 2 tbs. olive oil
- 500g zucchini (courgette), rinsed and cut into 1cm thick slices
- 1 tbs. Gourmet Garden Mint
- 2 tbs. balsamic vinegar

In a large frying pan, heat the oil over moderately high heat until it is hot, not smoking, then sauté zucchini slices in batches with sea salt and pepper for 2 minutes each side or until they are golden and tender, stir in the mint and vinegar and warm through.

Garlic Mushrooms

SERVES 4

- 500g mushrooms
- 2 tbs. olive oil
- 1 tsp. Gourmet Garden Garlic
- ¼ cup fresh flat leaf parsley

Preheat oven to 180°C. Place mushrooms in a large baking dish, drizzle with oil and garlic, roast in oven for 15 minutes or until mushrooms are tender and browned lightly. Stir in parsley.

Optional: Substitute fresh parsley for 2 tbs. Gourmet Garden Parsley.

Tip: Cook close to serving.

Ginger & Coriander Carrots

SERVES 4

- 1 bunch baby carrots
- ½ cup (160g) honey
- 1 tbs. Gourmet Garden Ginger
- 1 tbs. Gourmet Garden Coriander

Trim 1 bunch baby carrots (or slice 6 carrots). Boil or steam for 3 minutes or until just tender. Drain well. Add honey, ginger and coriander. Toss to coat over a low heat for 1 minute. Serve immediately.

Fact: Studies prove that Coriander is a good source of antioxidants and contains more antioxidants per serve than most vegetables and many fruit. So adding just a little Coriander to your meals can give you an antioxidant boost.

Italian Peas

SERVES 6

- 2 tbs. olive oil
- 1 tsp. Gourmet Garden Garlic
- 450g frozen peas
- 1 tsp. chicken stock

Heat oil in a fry pan over medium heat. Stir in garlic, peas and sprinkle with stock. Season with pepper, cover and cook until peas are tender, about 4–5 minutes.

Fact: In the mid 1920s, Clarence Birdseye went on a hunting trip to Labrador, Canada. It was winter, the weather was bitterly cold, and Birdseye was fascinated how the Eskimos caught the fish and hung them outside in the sub-zero temperatures to freeze solid ... Birdseye went on to become the founder of the modern frozen food industry.

Minted Lemon Asparagus

SERVES 4

- *2½ tbs. lemon juice*
- *1 tsp. Gourmet Garden Mint*
- *450g asparagus, woody ends removed*
- *¼ cup crumbled feta cheese*

In a small bowl mix together the lemon juice and mint. Set aside. Bring a large pot of water to the boil. Place in asparagus for about 45 seconds, remove then plunge into a bowl of ice water to stop the cooking process. Drain the asparagus and place on a serving platter. Drizzle with lemon mixture and sprinkle cheese over the top.

Tip: When buying asparagus, look for a crisp green spear ... Fresh asparagus should exude a little juice when you press the base of the spear with your fingers.

Minty Peas

SERVES 4

- *2 cups fresh peas*
- *1 tbs. Gourmet Garden Mint*
- *1 tbs. lemon juice*

Boil your peas and instead of coating them in butter, try tossing through a squeeze of Gourmet Garden Mint with fresh lemon juice. *Herbal and Healthy!*

Optional: If not fresh, use frozen peas.

Fact: Just one serve of freshly frozen garden peas has more Vitamin C than two large apples, more fibre than a slice of wholemeal bread and more thiamine than a glass of whole milk!

Oven Baked Tomatoes

SERVES 3

- *3 vine ripened tomatoes*
- *3 tsp. Gourmet Garden Basil*
- *3 tbs. grated parmesan cheese*

Preheat oven to 200°C. Cut the tomatoes in half. Place in an ovenproof dish, cut side up. Season each with sea salt and pepper. Smooth basil over each and top with parmesan. Bake for 20 minutes.

Rosemary & Garlic Roasted Pumpkin

SERVES 4

- *500g butternut pumpkin (butternut squash), peeled and cut into chunks*
- *1 tbs. olive oil*
- *1 tbs. Gourmet Garden Rosemary*
- *1 tbs. Gourmet Garden Garlic*

Preheat oven to 180°C. Place pumpkin on a baking tray and brush with olive oil. Mix together rosemary and garlic and glaze pumpkin. Pop into oven and roast for 25 minutes or until pumpkin is nice and tender.

Tip: If you have leftover pumpkin, remove seeds and place in the crisper section in a sealed plastic bag.

Sautéed Mushrooms

SERVES 4

- *2 tbs. olive oil*
- *4 tsp. Gourmet Garden Chilli*
- *4 tsp. Gourmet Garden Garlic*
- *300g mushrooms, sliced*

Heat oil in a non-stick frying pan over medium heat. Mix together chilli and garlic and spread over mushrooms. Pan fry for 3–4 minutes or until cooked.

Snow Peas in Garlic Mint Butter

SERVES 8

- *200g snow peas (mange tout)*
- *1½ tbs. butter*
- *1 tsp. Gourmet Garden Garlic*
- *1 tsp. Gourmet Garden Mint*

Top and tail snow peas. Melt butter in a frying pan and then add garlic and mint. Stir in peas, sauté until just tender.

Spinach with Garlic

SERVES 4

- *2 tbs. butter*
- *1 tbs. Gourmet Garden Garlic*
- *500g baby spinach*

Melt butter in a large fry pan over medium heat until it melts. Add the garlic and cook for 1 minute or until just beginning to brown. Add the spinach leaves and while stirring cook for 4 minutes, until the leaves are dark and about a quarter of their size.

Zucchini Pesto Sticks

SERVES 4

- *4 medium sized zucchinis (courgettes), cut in half lengthways*
- *2 tbs. Gourmet Garden Basil*
- *¼ cup (40g) pine nuts*
- *½ cup grated parmesan cheese*

Preheat oven to 180°C. Place all zucchinis halves onto a baking tray. Spread cut side of zucchinis with basil. Top evenly with pine nuts, season before sprinkling with parmesan. Bake for 10–12 minutes or until cheese has melted and zucchini is nice and tender.

Tip: The best zucchinis are the small 12cm or under tender ones. Most chefs agree that any over 20cm are fit only for stuffing ... You decide!

Mains

These days, there are many different ethnic recipes that use unique combinations of herbs and spices when using beef. Vietnamese cooks will often use lemon grass, ginger and fish sauce. German cooks will marinate and roast beef in wine, peppercorns and ginger.

Each culture ends up with favourites, and that's fantastic as it's about creating what your family and friends enjoy eating.

Beef

Basil & Parmesan Steaks

SERVES 4

- *2 rib eye steaks (about 3cm thick)*
- *2 tbs. Gourmet Garden Basil*
- *3 tbs. grated parmesan cheese*
- *1 tbs. extra virgin olive oil*

Preheat heavy frying pan until hot. Cut into the side of each steak (minimising the width of the opening cut), forming a deep pocket (do not cut through). Mix basil and parmesan and stuff into pockets. Press closed and drizzle with oil. Place steaks carefully in the pan and cook for 10 minutes for medium doneness; turn once when you see juices on the surface of the steak. When done, remove, cover and let stand for 5–10 minutes. Cut beef into thick strips to serve.

Optional: Seal opening with a toothpick.

Braised Beef in Chilli & Coconut

SERVES 4

- *500g lean beef strips*
- *2 tbs. Gourmet Garden Chilli*
- *400ml coconut cream*
- *1 (600g) sweet potato, peeled and cubed*

Place beef in a non stick frypan or large saucepan and cook over a medium/high heat until browned on the outside. Combine chilli and coconut cream and add to beef. Add sweet potato chunks, reduce heat and simmer for 30 minutes or until potatoes are cooked through.

Optional: Serve with rice to soak up the flavoursome sauce and for more of a curry flavour add 2tsp. garam masala.

Garlic Pepper Steak

SERVES 6

- *1 tbs. olive oil*
- *2 tsp. Gourmet Garden Garlic*
- *1 tbs. coarsely ground black pepper*
- *6 sirloin steaks*

Preheat BBQ. In a bowl, mix together the olive oil, garlic and pepper. Score steaks and rub with the mixture. Place steaks on BBQ and cook for 3–4 minutes each side or until done to your liking.

Hint: Gourmet Garden Garlic is perfect for busy weekday cooking. It's easy to use in many recipes and offers a rich, beautiful flavour.

Moroccan Stew

SERVES 4

- *550g sweet potato, peeled and diced*
- *2 tbs. Gourmet Garden Moroccan Fresh Blend*
- *550g chuck steak, diced*
- *400g tin tomatoes*

Place all ingredients into a slow cooker and cook on high for 4 hours or low for 6 ... Delicious served with couscous.

Optional: If you want to quickly do this on the stovetop. Simply brown the meat in a saucepan over a medium/high heat add remaining ingredients, bring to the boil, reduce heat and simmer until potatoes are nice and tender. This is just as nice substituting harissa for Moroccan Fresh Blend.

Prosciutto Wrapped Veal

SERVES 4

This is sensational!

- *4 veal cutlets*
- *4 tsp. Gourmet Garden Basil*
- *4 slices prosciutto*
- *½ cup (130g) whole egg mayonnaise*

Preheat oven to 200°C. Line baking tray with baking paper. Coat each cutlet with half the basil before wrapping with prosciutto. Place on baking tray and roast uncovered for 20 minutes or until cutlets are done to your liking. Meanwhile, mix together remaining basil and mayo until smooth. Serve cutlets dolloped with basil mayonnaise.

Tip: Gourmet Garden Basil is divine stirred through creamy pastas or spread over pizza bases too.

Rissoles

SERVES 4

- *500g lean mince*
- *2 large potatoes, boiled and mashed*
- *½ onion, finely chopped*
- *1 tbs. Gourmet Garden Italian Herbs*

Mix all ingredients in a bowl, season with sea salt and pepper. Once combined, shape into patties. Heat a non-stick frying pan and cook for 3–4 minutes each side or until a crusty brown exterior forms all over.

Optional: Serve with gravy and vegetables. The lovely Prue Blake will often coat her rissoles in flour before cooking them.

Roast Beef

SERVES 4–6

- *1 kg roast beef*
- *1 tbs. olive oil*
- *1 tbs. Gourmet Garden Garlic*
- *1 tbs. Gourmet Garden Oregano*

Preheat oven to 180°C. Brush beef all over with oil and herbs. Place beef in an oven bag, and close with the tie provided. Pierce 3 or 4 holes in top of bag near tie-end. Place into a roasting dish and cook for 50 minutes for medium doneness. Remove from oven, cover loosely with foil and rest for 10 minutes before slicing to serve.

Tip: Use the yummy juice to make a savoury gravy. Simply pour into a saucepan, add a little cornflour mixed with water to form a paste, stir until gravy thickens, season to taste.

Spicy Steak

SERVES 2

- ½ tsp. Gourmet Garden Garlic
- 1 tsp. curry powder
- 1 tsp. Gourmet Garden Coriander
- 2 rib fillets

Mix together first 3 ingredients and coat the steaks. Cover and marinate for at least 30 minutes. On a hot, oiled grill or BBQ, cook steaks for 3-4 minutes each side or until done to you liking. Let the steaks sit for 5 minutes before slicing thinly across the grain.

Optional: Serve with you favourite salad.

Steak with Mushroom & Garlic Sauce

SERVES 4

This is so easy and always a hit!

- 4 steaks
- 1 cup sliced mushrooms
- ⅔ cup (200ml) thickened cream
- ½ tsp. Gourmet Garden Garlic

Preheat a large non-stick frying pan to hot. Cook first sides of steak until moisture appears (approx. 3–4 minutes), turn and cook for another 3–4 minutes for a medium steak. Remove from pan, cover with foil and rest for 5 minutes. Meanwhile, place mushrooms in the steak residue and cook until just soft. Add cream and garlic and simmer until reduced and thickened. Season with sea salt and pepper.

Optional: Substituting garlic for fresh sage adds a lovely flavour too.

Steak Burgundy

SERVES 2

- *2 good-sized rib fillet steaks*
- *½ tbs. butter*
- *1 cup (250ml) red wine*
- *1 tsp. Gourmet Garden Garlic*

Preheat oven to 180°C. Marinate steaks in red wine for 2 hours then place each steak in an envelope of foil ensuring you have plenty to twist the top over to seal. Mix butter and garlic together and place an equal dollop on top of each steak. Seal the steak in by folding over foil. Place on a baking tray and bake in oven for 45 minutes. YUM. YUM. YUM!

Optional: Serve with roast vegetables or your favourite salad.

Thai Beef Stir-Fry

SERVES 4

- *500g stir-fry beef*
- *2 tbs. Gourmet Garden Thai Fresh Blend*
- *2 tbs. sesame oil*
- *2 spring onions, sliced*

Mix meat and Thai Blend together, cover and chill for 20 minutes. Heat oil in a wok or frying pan, then stir-fry meat in batches for 1 minute or until cooked on the outside and medium on the inside. Trim the spring onions and cut into thin lengthwise strips. Quickly stir-fry in wok. Serve meat on top of a salad (even just shredded ice-berg lettuce is nice) and top with spring onions and jus.

Optional: Vegetables that compliment a Thai stir-fry are baby corn, snow peas, red pepper (capsicum), bamboo shoots and water chestnuts.

Chicken

Chicken is rated as a very good source of protein, providing 67.6% of the daily value of protein in 125g. It is one of the most googled ingredients in the world and is really very easy to find new and unique ways to prepare.

Chicken marries beautifully with lemon pepper, garlic, marjoram, oregano, parsley, rosemary, tarragon and thyme ... Hope this inspires!

Asian Chicken

SERVES 4

- *600g chicken tender loins*
- *2 tbs. Gourmet Garden Lemon Grass*
- *2 tbs. sweet chilli sauce with ginger*
- *500g pkt snap frozen Asian vegetables*

Combine chicken and lemon grass and cook in a hot wok in batches, then set aside. Stir-fry vegies and chilli sauce and a ¼ cup (60ml) of water for 3 minutes. Return chicken to wok with vegies and stir-fry for a further 3–5 minutes.

Optional: Serve with noodles.

Chilli & Lime Chicken Wings

SERVES 4

- *500g chicken wings*
- *1 lime*
- *1 tbs. Gourmet Garden Garlic*
- *2 tbs. Gourmet Garden Chilli*

Preheat oven to 180°C. Remove chicken wing tips. Cut wings in two at the elbow joint and arrange in a single layer on a baking sheet. Bake for approx. 20 minutes or until almost done. Meanwhile, combine the juice of the lime with garlic and chilli. Remove wings from oven and turn. Brush the wings with the mixture, return to the oven and bake for approx. 10 minutes or until browned, basting every couple of minutes. Remove wings and cool slightly before serving.

Creamy Chives & Garlic Chicken

SERVES 4

- *200g cream cheese, softened*
- *1 tbs. Gourmet Garden Chives*
- *1 tsp. Gourmet Garden Garlic*
- *4 skinless boneless chicken breasts, butterflied*

Preheat oven to 180°C. In a bowl, mix the cream cheese, chives and garlic. Divide into balls. Place each ball in the centre of each chicken breast half, fold the chicken over the cream cheese and secure with toothpicks. Arrange the chicken in a baking dish and bake, covered with foil, for 20 minutes. Uncover, and bake for a further 10 minutes.

Optional: Serve with your favourite mash and vegetables.

Garlic & Rosemary Baked Chicken

SERVES 2

- *1 tsp. Gourmet Garden Garlic*
- *1 tbs. Gourmet Garden Rosemary*
- *1 tbs. lemon juice*
- *2 chicken thighs*

Preheat oven to 190°C. In a small bowl, mix together the garlic, rosemary, lemon juice and a little zest, season with sea salt and pepper. Rub over chicken and place in a baking dish, bake for 25 minutes. Baking time will depend on the thickness of your chicken.

Optional: Serve with roast vegetables or a delicious green salad.

Tip: Garlic is best added to dishes at the beginning of the cooking process to allow its flavour time to develop.

Herb Infused Roast Chicken

SERVES 6

- *1 chicken (size 16)*
- *¼ cup (55g) softened butter*
- *1 tbs. Gourmet Garden Garlic*
- *1 tbs. Gourmet Garden Oregano*

Preheat oven to 190°C. In a bowl, combine butter with the garlic and oregano. Very gently, lift up the skin on the underside of the chicken and stuff it with the butter mix. Use any remaining butter to rub all over the outside of the chicken. Season with sea salt and pepper. Place the chicken in the centre of the bag and tie. Pierce 3 or 4 holes in top of bag near the tie. Place in a baking tray and bake for approx. 40 minutes or until juices run clear. Serve with roast vegetables.

Optional: Add a heaped tablespoon of flour to the bag and shake to distribute. This helps make lovely gravy combined with the roasting juices.

Fact: The consumption of chicken has increased 6-fold from 1965 to today. As a kid in the 50s, my Mum can recall only ever eating Roast Chicken at Christmas time!

Honey & Lime Baked Drumsticks

MAKES 8

- *2 tbs. honey*
- *1 tbs. Gourmet Garden Coriander*
- *1 lime, juice and zest*
- *8 chicken drumsticks*

Combine first 3 ingredients in heat proof oven dish, add chicken, cover and refrigerate for 1 hour. Cook in a 200°C oven for 40 minutes basting throughout. Cover with foil if the drumsticks begin to colour too much. Serve with a lovely fresh, green salad.

Tip: Chicken drumsticks are great in casseroles, stews or baked in the oven. Score the flesh for faster cooking and remove the skin for a lower fat meal.

Mediterranean Chicken

SERVES 4

- *4 chicken fillet breasts*
- *100g Feta, crumbled*
- *2 tbs. Gourmet Garden Italian Herbs*
- *2 tbs. extra virgin olive oil*

Preheat oven to 200°C. Cut lengthways through each fillet to make a pocket (keeping the opening as narrow as possible), leaving 1 cm at each end. Mix together feta and Italian herbs before filling each pocket. Heat oil in a large frying pan over medium/high heat. Add chicken breasts and cook for 1–2 minutes or until golden on each side. Transfer to baking tray and roast for 7–10 minutes or until just cooked through. Cover and set aside to rest for 5 minutes before slicing to serve.

Optional: Serve with sweet potato mash and baby spinach.

Sweet & Spicy Chicken

SERVES 2

- *6 chicken legs*
- *½ cup (110g) orange marmalade*
- *1–2 tsp. Gourmet Garden Chilli*

Preheat oven to 180°C. Combine marmalade and chilli paste. Place chicken on a paper lined baking tray and rub glaze over each leg, coating well. Bake for 30–35 minutes or until done, glaze throughout.

Fact: A little known fact ... There are more chickens on earth than people.

Thai Chicken & Cashew Stir-fry

SERVES 4

- *500g chicken breast, thinly sliced*
- *2 tbs. Gourmet Garden Thai Fresh Blend*
- *1 large red pepper (capsicum), sliced*
- *50g cashews, roasted*

Coat chicken with Thai blend, cover and let marinate in the fridge for at least 30 minutes. Heat a non-stick wok, add a tbs. of water and stir-fry chicken for 2 minutes. Add pepper, stir, cover with lid and cook for a further 2–3 minutes or until done. Remove lid and stir through roasted cashews.

Optional: Serve over rice, garnished with some fresh coriander.

Tip: For another quick and easy stir-fry, combine Gourmet Garden Garlic, Chilli and Coriander with chicken, soy sauce and fresh Asian vegetables.

Fish & Seafood

Evidence is mounting that fish oil, rich in Omega 3, can help to prevent heart attacks. One of the clearest examples was identified in Japan. For years, doctors and researchers had been baffled by the low incidence of heart disease among the Japanese compared to Western countries. Studies found that the typical Japanese diet was high in fish and seafood. Similar findings were found among Inuits living in Greenland whose diet is almost exclusively fish, seal and whale.

Is fish good for you? Simply put ... VERY!

Baked Salmon with Parmesan Crust

SERVES 4

- 4 salmon steaks
- 2 tbs. Gourmet Garden Italian Herbs
- 125g parmesan cheese, finely grated
- 1 lemon

Sear salmon steaks on each side for 2 minutes, skin side down first. Meanwhile combine Italian herbs and the cheese. Spread this mixture over salmon steaks and squeeze fresh lemon juice over the top. Bake in a moderate oven for 15 minutes.

BBQ Marinated Calamari

SERVES 4

- ½ cup (125ml) olive oil
- ½ lemon, juiced
- ¾ tsp. Gourmet Garden Oregano
- 5 medium (about 100g each) cleaned squid hoods, cut into 5mm-thick rings

Combine oil, juice and oregano with a little sea salt and pepper. Place calamari into marinade and refrigerate for 2 hours, turning frequently. Preheat BBQ to hot, brush with a little oil and place the calamari on hot plate (it will curl). Cook for 1 minute, turn then cook for 1 more minute.

Fact: Fresh oregano is wild marjoram. It looks very similar to marjoram but has a stronger flavour. It is a popular ingredient in Italian, Mexican, Spanish and Mediterranean dishes just like this one.

Creamy Garlic Prawns

SERVES 4

A simple classic.

- 2 cups (370g) rice
- ⅔ cup (200ml) cream
- 1 tbs. Gourmet Garden Garlic
- 16 king prawns (shrimp), peeled and deveined

Boil rice, then rinse under hot water. Meanwhile, place garlic and cream in a wok or fry pan and reduce. Add prawns and cook until orange in colour. Serve on a bed of rice.

Fact: Never freeze garlic as it will kill the flavour.

Malaysian Fish Curry

SERVES 4

Enjoy the tastes of Asia with this creamy curry.

- *190g jar Malaysian curry paste*
- *400ml coconut milk*
- *2 tbs. Gourmet Garden Lemon Grass*
- *500g fresh fish fillets, cut into 3 cm pieces*

Combine curry paste and coconut milk in a wok or saucepan and bring to the boil. Add lemon grass and simmer for 5 minutes. Add fish cubes and simmer for 5–6 minutes or until soft.

Optional: Serve with steamed rice and garnish with fresh coriander.

Tip: Gourmet Garden Lemon Grass adds a subtle deliciousness to Asian stir-fries, laksas or curries.

Maple & Mustard Glazed Salmon

SERVES 4

- *4 salmon fillets, skin on*
- *2 tbs. wholegrain mustard*
- *1 tbs. maple syrup*
- *1 tsp. Gourmet Garden Garlic*

Preheat grill on high. Mix together the mustard, maple syrup and garlic. Place salmon skin side down in a baking dish or on a shallow tray that has been lined with foil. Spread the mustard mixture evenly over the tops of the salmon fillets. Grill for 10 minutes or until cooked through.

Optional: Serve with seasonal vegetables or salad.

Mediterranean Baked Fish

SERVES 6

- *6 x 200g white fish*
- *6 Roma tomatoes, cut into quarters*
- *⅓ cup (80ml) balsamic vinegar*
- *3 tbs. Gourmet Garden Oregano*

Preheat oven to 200°C. Place fish in a baking dish. In a large bowl mix tomato, balsamic and oregano. Spread evenly over the fish, season with sea salt and pepper and bake for 15–20 minutes or until cooked.

Minted Apricot Fish

SERVES 6

- *6 large white fish fillets*
- *425g apricot nectar*
- *30g pkt French onion soup*
- *1 tbs. Gourmet Garden Mint*

Preheat oven to 180°C. Combine the apricot nectar, soup mix and mint. Place fish in a baking dish and pour over apricot mixture. Cover and bake for 30–40 minutes.

Optional: Serve with a little lemon juice squeezed over the top.

Moroccan Salmon

SERVES 2

This is divine, everyone we serve this to requests the recipe.

- *2 salmon steaks*
- *1 tsp. olive oil*
- *1 tbs. Gourmet Garden Moroccan Fresh Blend*
- *1 tbs. Dukkah*

Preheat oven to 160°C. Place salmon on a non-stick baking tray. Coat each fillet lightly first with oil, then with Moroccan blend, sprinkle with dukkah and bake for 15 minutes or to your liking.

Optional: Substitute Moroccan Fresh Blend for harissa. Harissa is a Tunisian hot, red paste made from chillies and red peppers (capsicums) and flavoured with cloves, cumin and coriander.

Mussels in White Wine

SERVES 4

- *1¼ cups (300ml) white wine*
- *900g mussels, cleaned*
- *1 tbs. Gourmet Garden Parsley*
- *2 tbs. (30g) butter*

Melt butter in a large pan. Pour in wine and bring to the boil. Add mussels and cover the pan with lid. Cook over medium heat for 4–5 minutes; lightly shake the pan every minute. Remove mussels with tongs onto serving dish (leaving liquid) and discard any mussels that are still closed. Bring the remaining liquid to the boil. Season with sea salt and pepper and stir in parsley. Pour liquid over the mussels and serve immediately.

Prawn & Chorizo Skewers

MAKES 20

- 4 chorizo sausages
- 40 medium green prawns (shrimp), peeled, tails left on
- 1 tbs. Gourmet Garden Italian Herbs
- 1 tbs. olive oil

Preheat BBQ to hot. If using wooden skewers, soak them in water for at least 30 minutes before using to prevent burning. Peel and cut each chorizo into 10 round slices. Grill or fry each side for 1 minute. Skewer a prawn around a chorizo slice. Repeat the process then do the same with the other 19 skewers. Season with salt and pepper, brush with Italian herbs and oil, grill on the BBQ for 2 minutes each side or until prawns are just cooked.

Tip: Always deep or pan fry fish and seafood in clean oil as it will flavour the oil and taint any other foods fried in it.

Salmon & Herbs in Prosciutto Parcels

SERVES 4

- 4 salmon steaks, skinless
- 4 slices prosciutto
- 2 tsp. Gourmet Garden Coriander
- 2 tsp. Gourmet Garden Dill

Preheat oven to 180°C. Divide herbs among salmon fillets and smear over top. Wrap in prosciutto, place on a paper lined baking tray and bake for 20–25 minutes.

Optional: Serve with lemon wedges. Replace dill with garlic, and combine both coriander and garlic for a lovely paste with which to flavour the fish.

Steamed Garlic Mussels

SERVES 4

- *410g can diced tomatoes*
- *2 tsp. Gourmet Garden Garlic*
- *2 kg small black mussels*
- *2 tbs. chopped parsley*

Place tinned tomatoes, garlic and ½ cup of water in a large saucepan and bring to boil. Reduce heat and simmer uncovered for about 5 minutes. Meanwhile, clean mussels and remove beards. Add mussels to pan and shaking occasionally, simmer covered for 5 minutes or until mussels open (discard any that don't open). Remove mussels and keep warm. Bring tomato mixture to the boil and cook uncovered for 5 minutes or until mixture thickens. Gently stir in parsley before returning mussels.

Optional: Serve with freshly baked crusty bread.

Steamed Ginger Fish

SERVES 4

- *4 fresh ocean fish fillets*
- *1 tbs. Gourmet Garden Ginger*
- *Drizzle of soy sauce*
- *1 shredded spring onion*

Arrange fish in a steamer basket, spread with ginger and drizzle with soy sauce. Place steamer basket over a pan of simmering water and cover tightly. Steam fish for 6–8 minutes or until cooked. Drizzle fish with extra soy and top with shredded green onion. Serve with steamed Asian greens and rice.

Tip: Gourmet Garden Ginger — combine with soy sauce to marinate fish or stir through steamed carrots.

Stir-Fried Prawns

SERVES 4

- *2 tbs. sesame oil*
- *2 tbs. Gourmet Garden Thai Fresh Blend*
- *500g peeled prawns (shrimp)*
- *50g rice vermicelli, boiled*

Heat oil in a large saucepan over medium heat. Add Thai Blend and prawns and cook until prawns turn orange, toss through vermicelli to coat.

Optional: Add some Bok Choy at the end for a little green.

Lamb

Lamb is an excellent source of high quality protein. It is an ideal source of iron, it provides 45% of the daily requirement of zinc and it is a great source of B vitamins.

The following herbs go well with lamb: Basil, bay leaf, caraway, coriander, cumin, dill, marjoram, rosemary, sage, and thyme.

Balsamic Glazed Lamb Cutlets

SERVES 4

Delicious, quick and healthy too!

- *12 lamb cutlets*
- *2 tbs. balsamic vinegar*
- *2 tbs. honey*
- *1 tbs. Gourmet Garden Rosemary*

Heat frypan, grill or BBQ. Mix last 3 ingredients. Cook cutlets for 1–2 minutes each side or until just starting to brown. Brush with baste and cook a further 3 minutes each side, basting occasionally. Serve drizzled with the tasty jus.

Tip: Rosemary adds delicious taste to a range of dishes. Part of the mint family and originally from the Mediterranean, rosemary is perfect rubbed on lamb, pork or chicken before barbequing or roasting.

Greek Style Roast Lamb

SERVES 4

- *1½ kg leg of lamb*
- *½ cup (125ml) olive oil*
- *¼ cup (60ml) lemon juice*
- *2 tbs. Gourmet Garden Oregano*

Combine the oil, lemon juice, oregano with sea salt and pepper in a large non metallic dish. Add leg of lamb and coat well with marinade. Cover and let sit in refrigerator for 2 hours or if time allows, overnight. In a roasting tray, bake in a preheated 180°C oven for 1–1½ hours or until done to your liking. Remove from oven, cover loosely with foil and sit for 15 minutes before carving.

Optional: Slice and serve with pita bread, tzatziki and tabouli salad.

Lamb Racks with Mustard Glaze

SERVES 4

- *2 tsp. Gourmet Garden Garlic*
- *⅓ cup (80g) maple syrup*
- *2 tbs. Dijon mustard*
- *4 x 4 lamb racks*

Preheat oven to 180°C. Place garlic, maple syrup and mustard in a small bowl and mix well to combine. Line a baking tray with baking paper. Place lamb racks on paper and brush generously each with mustard mixture. Roast uncovered for 20 minutes or until done to your liking.

Lamb & Mint Patties

MAKES 8

Y.U.M.M.Y

- *500g lamb mince*
- *½ onion, finely diced*
- *1 tbs. Gourmet Garden Mint*
- *2 tbs. sweet chilli sauce*

Combine all ingredients and season with sea salt and pepper. Form into rissoles and cook in a non-stick frying pan for 4–5 minutes each side or until nice and crunchy on the outside.

Optional: These are delicious served with a dollop of Raita (see: 4 Ingredients 2) or extra sweet chilli sauce to dip.

Mediterranean Char-Grilled Lamb

SERVES 4

- *500g lamb back straps*
- *2 zucchinis (courgettes)*
- *1 red pepper (capsicum), quartered and deseeded*
- *1 tbs. Gourmet Garden Rosemary*

Place lamb in a medium/hot non-stick frying pan and cook for 4 minutes each side or until done to your liking. Remove from heat and sit for 5 minutes. Meanwhile, cut the zucchini in half and then slice lengthways and similarly slice the pepper, then place into the jus of the lamb and lightly sauté. After 2 minutes, coat with rosemary and season. Cook for a further 2 minutes or until tender. Slice the lamb and toss through vegetables.

Optional: Serve on a bed of rocket drizzled with a little balsamic vinegar.

Moroccan Lamb with Shiraz & Honey Sauce

SERVES 4

- 1 (10 bone) rack of lamb, trimmed (ask your butcher)
- 2 tbs. Gourmet Garden Moroccan Fresh Blend
- 1 cup (250ml) shiraz
- ⅓ cup (100g) honey

Preheat oven to 200°C. Season lamb with sea salt and rub with Moroccan blend. In an oven proof fry pan over medium/high heat, sear lamb on all sides until evenly browned. Place lamb in the oven and roast for 30–40 minutes or until done to your liking. Remove lamb from fry pan reserving juices and allow to rest for 10–15 minutes before slicing. Place fry pan with juices over medium heat and stir in wine and honey. Cook until reduced by half and drizzle over ribs to serve.

Optional: Serve with couscous or vegetables and use harissa instead of Moroccan Fresh Blend for a different flavour.

Moroccan Lamb Koftas

SERVES 4

Enjoy the tastes of Africa with these delicious kebabs.

- *500g minced lamb*
- *2 tbs. Gourmet Garden Moroccan Fresh Blend*
- *1 small onion, finely diced*
- *1 tbs. olive oil*

Combine the mince, Moroccan blend, onion and season with salt and pepper. Using metal skewers, gently squeeze enough of the mixture along the skewer to cover the top half. This should resemble a fat sausage. Heat the oil on a BBQ plate or frying pan over medium/high and cook, turning frequently for about 15 minutes.

Optional: Serve with couscous and cucumber yoghurt. Substitute Moroccan Fresh Blend for harissa.

Roast Lamb

MAKES 4

- *1½ kg leg of lamb*
- *1 sprig rosemary*
- *1 tbs. Gourmet Garden Garlic*
- *2 tbs. olive oil*

Preheat oven to 200°C. Cut a 2 cm slit across the lamb in several places and insert 6 rosemary leaves and rub over with garlic. Coat the baking dish with oil and bake for 1 hour or until done.

Optional: Serve with roast vegetables and gravy or sliced on a fresh crusty roll.

Hint: With any roast lamb, the flavour can be enhanced by adding fresh mint to the slits prior to roasting.

Pasta

*The word pasta comes from the Italian word meaning 'paste'
a combination of flour and water.*

*The real pleasure of using herbs in pasta is the ease by which you can
conjure dishes of terrific freshness and taste. In particular basil, garlic,
mint, oregano, rosemary and thyme compliment pasta well.*

Crab Spaghetti

SERVES 4

- *400g spaghetti*
- *300g cooked crab meat*
- *500g jar tomato and herb pasta sauce*
- *1 tbs. Gourmet Garden Garlic*

Cook pasta in boiling water until al dente. Set aside and keep warm.
Add the crab meat, pasta sauce and parsley to saucepan and bring
to the boil. Reduce heat and simmer for 5 minutes, season to taste.
Add the spaghetti and stir to combine. Divide among serving plates
and serve with crusty bread.

*Optional: Tinned crab or fresh prawns (shrimp) can be easily
substituted for fresh crab.*

Garlic Bread

SERVES 4–6

A lovely, warm garlic bread with any pasta is divine, this is no exception!

- *½ cup unsalted butter*
- *2 tsp. Gourmet Garden Garlic*
- *1 tbs. Gourmet Garden Parsley*
- *1 French stick*

Mix together the first three ingredients and season with sea salt and pepper. Slice the bread ¾ through and spread each slice generously with butter mix. Wrap in foil and bake in a 180°C oven for 10 minutes, unwrap foil and bake for a further 2–3 minutes to add a little crunch to the top of the bread. Slice through to serve.

Greek Spaghetti

SERVES 4

- *400g spaghetti*
- *6 tbs. butter*
- *1 cup grated parmesan cheese*
- *1 tsp. Gourmet Garden Oregano*

Preheat oven to 120°C. Bring a large pot of salted water to the boil. Add pasta and cook for 10 minutes or until done, drain. In a medium fry pan, melt butter with ½ tsp. salt and cook until just brown. Remove from heat and toss with pasta, cheese and oregano. Pour into a baking dish and bake for 10–15 minutes or until hot and bubbly.

Optional: Try using the Greek style parmesan called 'kefalaki' if available in your local supermarket or delicatessen.

Lemon Basil Pasta

SERVES 4

- *400g spaghetti*
- *2 tbs. olive oil*
- *3 tbs. lemon juice*
- *2 tbs. Gourmet Garden Basil*

Bring a large pot of salted water to a boil. Add pasta and cook for 10 minutes or until done, drain. In a small bowl combine olive oil, lemon juice, basil and ½ tsp. ground black pepper. Mix well and toss with the pasta. Serve hot or cold.

Matriciana

SERVES 4

- *400g spaghetti*
- *4 bacon rashers, chopped*
- *700g jar pasta sauce*
- *1–2 tsp. Gourmet Garden Chilli*

Cook pasta as per packet instructions then drain. In a non-stick frying pan, fry bacon until just done. Reduce heat to low and mix in pasta sauce and chilli, simmer over a low heat for 5 minutes. Mix through pasta and serve with slices of fresh crusty bread.

Mediterranean Prawn Linguini

SERVES 4

- *400g linguini*
- *250g green prawns (shrimp), peeled*
- *3 tbs. of Gourmet Garden Italian Herbs*
- *1 punnet cherry tomatoes, cut in half*

Boil linguini in a pot of salted boiling water for 8 minutes or until al dente, drain. Meanwhile, heat a frying pan over medium heat, add prawns coated in Italian herbs. Reduce heat, add the tomatoes, season and toss until prawns are orange and tomatoes soft. Turn the heat off and toss through linguini.

Pasta with Crab & Lemon Cream Sauce

SERVES 4

- *500g spiral pasta*
- *300ml cream*
- *2 tbs. Gourmet Garden Lemon Grass*
- *400g freshly cooked crab meat (or 2 x 170g tin crab meat, drained)*

Bring water to the boil. Add pasta and cook until tender. Meanwhile, add cream and lemon grass to a medium sized saucepan and bring to the boil. Reduce heat, add crabmeat and stir gently until heated through. Remove from heat and pour over pasta.

Optional: This is really nice with ¼ cup of freshly chopped flat leaf parsley mixed through it and sprinkled with a little lemon zest if you have one in your fridge.

Quick Pasta Sauce

SERVES 6

- *2 tbs. olive oil*
- *1 tbs. Gourmet Garden Garlic*
- *1 tbs. Gourmet Garden Basil*
- *700g bottle passata*

In a large non-stick frying pan over medium heat, sauté garlic in oil until tender, approx. 1 minute. Stir in basil and passata. Season with sea salt and pepper and cook for 15–20 minutes until slightly thickened. Serve immediately over your favourite pasta.

Tip: Passata it is just pure tomatoes, pureed and strained. It is unseasoned so very useful, for sauces, soups, pizza, lasagne and nearly anything you use tomatoes in. Add herbs, sugar or whatever your family will enjoy eating.

Ricotta Spaghetti

SERVES 4

- *350g spaghetti*
- *1 tsp. Gourmet Garden Garlic*
- *1 cup ricotta cheese*
- *1 tbs. Gourmet Garden Basil*

Fill a large pot with lightly salted water and bring to the boil. Stir in spaghetti and cook until al dente, stirring occasionally. Drain well, reserving ½ cup of liquid. Stir the garlic, ricotta and basil in a saucepan over low/medium heat for 4 minutes or until hot. Season to taste with sea salt and pepper, stir in the spaghetti, gradually add reserved water until desired consistency is reached.

Optional: Italian friends often made this for us and would substitute basil with a healthy serving of fresh flat-leaf parsley.

Marinara Sauce

SERVES 4

- 700g jar tomato pasta sauce
- ½ cup (125ml) dry white wine
- 1 kg fresh marinara mix
- 2 tbs. Gourmet Garden Basil

Combine pasta sauce, wine and 1 cup (250ml) of water in a saucepan and bring to the boil. Reduce heat and simmer uncovered for 10 minutes. Cook seafood in a separate frying pan on high for 3 minutes. Add to pasta sauce along with basil and gently simmer, allowing time for flavours to develop.

Optional: Serve over your family's favourite pasta.

Spinach Garlic Pasta

SERVES 6–8

- 450g angel hair pasta
- 1 tbs. olive oil
- 2 tsp. Gourmet Garden Garlic
- 285g frozen spinach, thawed

Cook the pasta in a large pot of salted boiling water until al dente, drain. Heat oil in a large fry pan, add garlic, spinach and the pasta and season. Mix well and cook for approx. 2 minutes, stirring often. Serve with crusty bread.

Tip: See 4 Ingredients Fast, Fresh & Healthy for ways to make your very own homemade pastas.

Spaghetti Al Olio

SERVES 4–6

- 450g spaghetti
- ¾ cup (180ml) olive oil
- 1 tbs. Gourmet Garden Garlic
- 1 tbs. Gourmet Garden Italian Herbs

Bring a large pot of lightly salted water to the boil and cook the pasta for about 10 minutes or until al dente, drain, reserving ½ cup of liquid. Meahwhile, place oil in a fry pan over medium heat, add garlic and sauté for 1 minute or until just brown. Remove from heat. Add remaining oil along with Italian herbs. Stir for 1 minute. In a bowl, combine oil, reserved liquid and spaghetti and mix well. Season with sea salt and pepper before serving.

Hint: In Italian 'Al Olio' means 'with oil'.

Spaghetti with Garlic & Basil

SERVES 6

- 500g spaghetti
- ½ cup (115g) unsalted butter
- 2 tsp. Gourmet Garden Garlic
- 1½ tbs. Gourmet Garden Basil

Bring a large pot of salted water to a boil and cook spaghetti for 10 minutes or until al dente, drain. In a small fry pan melt the butter, add the garlic and basil, cook stirring for 1 minute. In a large bowl toss the spaghetti with the butter and herbs, season with sea salt and pepper. Serve topped with parmesan cheese if desired.

Tip: 1 cup of cooked spaghetti provides about 200 calories, 40 grams of carbohydrates, less than 1 gram of total fat, no cholesterol and only 1 gram of sodium.

Pork

Pork is big business, it is the world's most widely eaten meat.

It is rather apt that it is responsible for the naming of one of the world's leading financial centres. To stop free roaming pigs rampaging through their grain fields, Manhattan Island residents built a long wall on the northern edge of what is now lower Manhattan.

*The street that ran along the wall was named ... **Wall Street!***

BBQ Spare Ribs

SERVES 6

- *500g pork spare ribs*
- *Olive oil cooking spray*
- *375ml BBQ sauce*
- *1 tbs. Gourmet Garden Ginger*

Into a large saucepan place ribs, cover with water and bring to the boil. Reduce heat and simmer for 10 minutes or until cooked. Drain and place on a lightly oiled baking tray. Mix together sauce and ginger before generously coating the ribs. Bake in a preheated 170°C oven for 20 minutes, turning once, or until brown and sticky.

Dill & Honey Pork Chops

SERVES 6

These are just lovely.

- *1 tbs. olive oil*
- *6 thick pork chops*
- *2 tbs. honey*
- *1 tsp. Gourmet Garden Dill*

Heat a fry pan over medium high and add oil. Pan fry chops for
3 minutes then turn for another 3 minutes. Remove from heat.
In a bowl, mix together honey and dill and coat each chop. Place
chops back in the pan and cook for 1 minute each side or until done to
your likeness. Serve drizzled with the tasty jus.

*Tip: Reserve a little of the yummy glaze to apply in the last 5 minutes
of cooking. To ensure the glaze doesn't burn, place a piece of baking
paper in the pan prior to cooking.*

Grilled Sausages with Tomato Stew

SERVES 6-8

- *8 Italian flavoured sausages*
- *350g jar passata*
- *1 tbs. Gourmet Garden Italian Herbs*
- *400g can lentils, drained*

Grill sausages until cooked, remove from heat and allow to rest. In the
same frying pan, cook the passata and Italian herbs, season and bring
to the boil. Reduce heat, add the lentils and simmer for 10 minutes.
Serve with sliced sausages mixed through the stew.

Optional: Fresh lentils are also nice.

Italian Style Pork Chops

SERVES 4

- 4 pork chops
- 2 tsp. Gourmet Garden Garlic
- 400g tin of oregano and basil tomatoes
- ½ cup (125ml) cream

In a non-stick pan fry pork until golden on both sides, add tinned tomatoes, bring to boil then gently simmer for 2½ hours (you may need a little more tomato mixture, depending on size of fillets). Half an hour before serving, add cream and increase heat to thicken.

Optional: Serve with mashed potatoes and steamed beans.

Tip: Gourmet Garden Garlic — cooked in casseroles, stews, roast meats and poultry is extremely versatile.

Mediterranean Grilled Sausages

SERVES 6

- 12 Italian flavoured pork sausages
- 1 tbs. Gourmet Garden Italian Herbs
- 2 vine-ripened tomatoes, diced into smallish pieces
- 100g goats cheese

In a non-stick pan fry sausages for 5 minutes, piercing a hole in their skins half way through. Remove from heat and lay on a foil lined tray. Allow to cool slightly before cutting in half lengthways. Press gently to flatten, smear a layer of Italian herbs over each half, top with tomatoes, season and sprinkle with bits of broken goats' cheese. Bake in a 180°C oven for 10 minutes or until the edges of the cheese are golden and the tomatoes are warmed through and slightly wilted.

Orange & Ginger Glaze

MAKES 1 CUP

- ¾ cup (185ml) orange marmalade
- 2 tsp. lemon juice
- ½ tsp. Gourmet Garden Ginger
- ½ tsp. dry mustard

Simply mix together all the ingredients and use to glaze your favourite cut of roast pork. This is particularly nice served as a glaze for pork belly or Christmas hams.

Pork & Potatoes in Red Wine

SERVES 4

- 4 pork chops
- 700g waxy potatoes, peeled and cubed
- 1 tsp. Gourmet Garden Coriander
- 1½ cups (375ml) red wine

Trim the fat from chops and melt in a non-stick fry pan. Add potatoes and cook over med-low heat for 15 minutes or until golden brown, stirring occasionally. Remove and transfer to a casserole dish. Add chops to fry pan and cook over medium heat turning occasionally for 8 minutes. Transfer to casserole dish. Gently stir in coriander, salt, pepper and ⅓ cup (80ml) water and red wine. Place in preheated 180°C oven and cook for 1 hour.

Optional: Serve with green beans.

*Tip: Most people will be familiar with this kind of dish known as **Afelia** (essentially pork stewed with red wine) a simple but delicious Greek dish ... Try it!*

Roast Pork

SERVES 8

- 2 kg roast leg of pork
- 3 tbs. extra virgin olive oil
- 1 tbs. Gourmet Garden Lemon Grass

Preheat oven to 220°C. Rub 1 tbs. oil onto rind of pork and then the lemon grass. Grind sea salt over rind and rub into pork. Pour remaining oil into baking dish and place in oven for 20 minutes. Reduce heat to 180°C and cook for 1¼ hours (or half hour per 500g).

Optional: Kim's husband, Glen scores the skin and bathes it with fresh lemon juice and loads of ground sea salt making a divine crackling!

San Choy Bow

SERVES 4

These are light and lovely.

- 500g pork mince
- 2 tbs. Gourmet Garden Thai Fresh Blend
- 1 carrot, grated
- 8 iceberg lettuce leaves

Mix Thai blend and carrots into mince and stir-fry in a hot wok until cooked. Divide mixture among lettuce leaves.

Optional: Serve with sweet chilli sauce to dip.

Vegetarian Mains

There are 6.5 billion people in the world.

*Approximately 1.6 billion of these people will have a mostly vegetarian diet — that is **a quarter** of the world's population.*

Asparagus & Lemon Risotto

SERVES 4–6

- *2 cups (370g) short grain rice*
- *340g can asparagus spears*
- *1 ltr. vegetable stock*
- *3 tbs. Gourmet Garden Lemon Grass*

Rinse the rice and set aside. Drain the asparagus, retaining juice (approx. ½ a cup). Mix together juice and stock in a large saucepan and bring to the boil. In a large frying pan, add rice and 1 cup of broth, stir constantly until broth is absorbed. Add ½ cup of broth and stir until absorbed. Stir in asparagus and lemon grass. Add remaining broth, ½ cup at a time, stirring constantly until each portion of broth is absorbed before adding the next (about 10 minutes). Remove from heat. Season to taste, add a little more lemon grass if desired.

Optional: Chives and parsley combine with the rind of lemon to add beautiful flavour to risottos, as does asparagus, mint and lemon.

Tip: Risotto is traditionally made with Arborio rice because of its high starch content and firm texture. Constant stirring helps release the rice's starches, creating a creamy texture with separate grains.

Baked Potato with Tomato Salsa

SERVES 1

- *1 large potato (250g)*
- *¼ cup (55g) cottage cheese*
- *2 tbs. tomato salsa*
- *½ tsp. Gourmet Garden Chives*

Preheat oven to 180°C. Pierce potato with knife several times. Wrap in foil and bake for 30 minutes or until soft. Remove from oven and stand for 5 minutes. Remove foil and cut a crisscross into the potato, half way through. Add cottage cheese, top with salsa and chives.

Filling options: *Sweet corn, parsley, cheddar cheese*
Sautéed red onion, mushrooms, pizza sauce, cheese
Hot baked beans topped with cheddar cheese
Sea salt, sour cream, smoked cheddar cheese, chives

Baked Ravioli

SERVES 4–6

- *500g vegetarian ravioli*
- *500g jar roasted vegetables pasta sauce*
- *2 tbs. Gourmet Garden Basil*
- *200g parmesan cheese, grated*

Preheat oven to 180°C. Cook ravioli in boiling water until just cooked, drain. Line a casserole dish with a layer of ravioli. Mix pasta sauce and basil together and spread over pasta. Sprinkle with a layer of cheese. Repeat layering process finishing with a layer of sauce topped with cheese. Bake for 15 minutes or until the cheese has melted.

Optional: Serve hot with salad, homemade potato chips or just by itself.

Corn & Chives Frittatas

SERVES 2

- *4 eggs, beaten*
- *½ cup grated cheese*
- *220g can creamed corn*
- *1 tbs. Gourmet Garden Chives*

Preheat oven to 180°C. Whisk all ingredients together and divide into four greased ramekins. Bake for 15 minutes or until golden brown.

Optional: Serve with crusty bread and a lovely fresh garden salad.

Gourmet Pizza

SERVES 4

- *2 pieces shortcrust pastry*
- *200g feta, crumbled*
- *150g semi-dried tomatoes, chopped*
- *1 tbs. Gourmet Garden Oregano*

Preheat oven to 180°C. Place shortcrust pastry on a paper lined baking tray and bake for 8 minutes. Remove and cool. Mix together remaining ingredients and season with pepper. Spread evenly over each pastry sheet and bake for 5–6 minutes or until the cheese slightly browns. Cut into triangular quarters to serve.

Optional: Add whatever toppings your family will eat ... This is a deliciously different way to make pizza!

Herbed Potato Frittatas

MAKES 12

- *1.5kg Desiree potatoes, washed and peeled*
- *2 tbs. Gourmet Garden Italian Herbs*
- *½ cup freshly chopped flat leaf parsley*
- *8 eggs, whisked*

Preheat oven to 180°C. In a saucepan of salted, boiling water place potatoes and cook for 20–25 minutes or until tender. Remove, drain and allow to cool. When cool, chop into small pieces and place in a large bowl. With a large, metal spoon gently fold through remaining ingredients and season. Pour the mixture evenly across 12 greased muffin tins and bake for 25 minutes or until set.

Optional: Serve with sweet chilli sauce and a wedge of lime. Substitute Italian Herbs for 1tbs. Gourmet Garden Rosemary.

Pasta with Basil

SERVES 4

- *2½ cups Risoni pasta*
- *1 small onion, chopped*
- *1 tbs. Gourmet Garden Basil*
- *1 cup Mozzarella cheese*

Cook pasta according to packet directions. Meanwhile in a non-stick fry pan, fry onion until tender. Stir in basil and cook for 1 minute. Drain pasta, add basil mixture and remove from heat. Stir in cheese until it begins to melt. Serve immediately.

Fact: Served in smaller quantities this is a great side dish with steak, chicken or fish.

Pea & Mint Omelette

SERVES 2

Delicious served with crusty bread and a fresh, garden salad for lunch or dinner.

- *½ cup fresh peas*
- *4 eggs*
- *1 tbs. Gourmet Garden Mint*
- *1 tbs. butter*

Cook the peas in a pan of salted boiling water for 2 minutes or until tender. Drain well and set aside. Beat eggs with a fork, season then add peas and mint and stir well. Heat butter in a non-stick frying pan until foamy, pour in mixture and cook over a medium heat for 3–4 minutes or until the mixture is nearly set. Complete by placing under a grill until golden and set.

Polenta Chips

SERVES 6

- *1 kg pkt. ready made polenta*
- *2 tbs. Gourmet Garden Rosemary*
- *2 tbs. Gourmet Garden Garlic*
- *100g parmesan cheese, grated*

Preheat oven to 200°C. Cut polenta into chip sizes. Mix together rosemary and garlic and coat polenta chips. Coat each with parmesan. Lay on a baking paper lined tray, season and bake for 20 minutes or until brown and crispy.

Optional: Serve with your favourite salad.

Thai Chickpea Patties

SERVES 4

- 300g can chickpeas
- 2 cups mashed potato
- 3 tbs. Gourmet Garden Thai Fresh Blend
- ½ cup freshly cut coriander

Pulse chickpeas in a food processor until roughly chopped. Transfer to a bowl. Add remaining ingredients. Season with pepper and stir until combined. Using a quarter cup measure, shape into 12 patties. Cook in a non-stick frying pan over medium heat. Cook patties for 3–4 minutes on each side or until golden.

Tip: The roots of coriander are incredibly flavoursome. In Thailand the roots are pounded with garlic to use as a paste and marinade for many dishes.

Thai Green Curry

SERVES 4

- 2 tbs. Gourmet Garden Lemon Grass
- 2 tbs. green curry paste
- 270ml can coconut cream
- 500g stir-fry Asian vegetables

Place lemon grass and curry paste into a non-stick frying pan and sauté over a medium heat until fragrant. Add coconut milk, ⅓ cup (80ml) water and vegetables. Simmer until vegetables are cooked through.

Optional: Serve over steamed rice to soak up the tasty sauce.

Tuscan Stuffed Peppers

SERVES 4

- 2 large red peppers (capsicums), cut in half
- ¼ loaf sour dough, torn
- 120g goats cheese, crumbled
- 2 tbs. Gourmet Garden Italian Herbs

Preheat oven to 180°C. Scrape out the peppers and place on a baking tray. Mix sour dough, goats cheese and Italian herbs and season with sea salt and pepper. Stuff pepper shells and bake for 40 minutes or until the pepper is nice and tender.

Optional: Drizzle all with a splash of olive oil prior to baking.

Desserts

Ever tried adding herbs to desserts?
*Ponder these **sensational** ideas.*
Rosemary, often found in cakes containing lemon peel or lemon curd
Mango Cheesecake with Basil Lime Syrup
Chocolate & Basil Mousse
Lavender Sugar (⅓ L : 1 S) as a base for baking

A general rule when using herbs in desserts is not to over do it,
as large doses will overwhelm the taste ... Bon appétit!

Almond Brittle with Rosemary

SERVES 4–6

This is sensational!

- *300g almonds*
- *1 tbs. Gourmet Garden Rosemary*
- *3 cups (660g) sugar*
- *1 tsp. white vinegar*

Preheat oven to 180°C. Line a baking tray with baking paper, place the almonds on and cook for 5 minutes or until lightly toasted. Set aside, cool and coat with rosemary. In a medium, heavy-based, clean saucepan, combine the sugar, 1 cup (250ml) water and vinegar. Cook over high heat until the sugar dissolves and then turns a light golden brown, about l5-20 minutes (be careful as the sugar can burn quickly). Once the caramel is off the heat, pour onto the baking tray, spreading evenly over the almonds. Allow the brittle to cool completely, break into pieces to serve or store in an air-tight container in your pantry.

Optional: This is lovely crushed and served sprinkled over ice-cream.

Basil & Lime Syrup

MAKES 1 CUP

- ½ cup (110g) sugar
- ½ cup (125ml) water
- 1 tsp. Gourmet Garden Basil
- 1 tbs. grated lime rind

Combine sugar and water in a saucepan and bring to a boil. Cook for 1 minute or until sugar dissolves. Remove from heat, stir in basil and lime rind. Cool. Strain and discard solids.

Optional: Substitute Gourmet Garden Basil for ½ cup of fresh basil leaves chopped.

Tip: This is DIVINE served over a mixture of fresh chunks of pineapple, mango, strawberries and kiwifruit.

Caramel Tart

SERVES 6

- 1 sheet short crust pastry
- 400g can Carnation caramel
- 1 cup (250ml) cold cream, whipped
- ⅔ tsp. Gourmet Garden Mint

Preheat oven to 180°C. Line a pie dish with baking paper and add the sheet of pastry, gently moulding it into the dish. Place in oven for 8–10 minutes, or until golden brown. Allow to cool before spooning in caramel. Spread mint over caramel and top with whipped cream. Smooth with the back of a warm dessertspoon … *As easy as 1,2,3,4!*

Optional: Substitute mint for rosemary.

Chocolate & Basil Ganache

- *150ml cream*
- *180g dark chocolate*
- *1 tsp. Gourmet Garden Basil*

Pop cream into a saucepan and bring to the boil. Remove from heat and add chocolate and basil, let sit for 3–4 minutes, then stir to combine. This is heavenly spread over freshly baked chocolate cake or fairy cakes.

Choc-Mint Candied Peel

SERVES 4–6

Serve as a tantalising after dinner treat!

- *2 oranges, quartered then peeled*
- *1 cup (200g) caster sugar*
- *150g dark chocolate*
- *½ tsp. Gourmet Garden Mint, brought to room temperature*

Using a peeler, peel rind lengthways into 1cm thick strips, place in a saucepan and cover with plenty of cold water. Bring to the boil and simmer for 5 minutes. Drain well. Return to pan and repeat the process. Combine boiled peel, 2 cups (500ml) of water and sugar in a saucepan. Cook over low heat stirring for 5 minutes until sugar dissolves. Increase heat and bring to the boil. Cook, stirring occasionally until the peel is translucent and tender. Drain and allow to cool. Melt chocolate in the microwave, stirring every 20 seconds before adding mint. Dip rind in chocolate, place on a paper lined baking tray and set in the fridge before serving.

Lychees in Mint & Ginger Syrup

SERVES 4

- ¾ cup (170g) caster sugar
- 1 tsp. Gourmet Garden Ginger
- 5 sprigs fresh mint
- 500g fresh lychees, peeled

Place the sugar and 1¼ cups (300ml) water in a medium saucepan. Stir over low heat until the sugar dissolves. Add the ginger and three mint sprigs. Increase heat to high and bring to the boil. Reduce heat to medium/low and simmer for 5 minutes. Add lychees and simmer for a further 4–5 minutes or until the lychees are tender. Remove the sprigs of mint and discard. Set aside and cool allowing time for the flavours to develop. Stir in the remaining mint, shredded, and serve.

Raspberry Mint Soft Serve

SERVES 4–6

- 2 cups fresh raspberries
- 1 tsp. Gourmet Garden Mint
- ½ cup (160g) Manuka honey
- 625g Greek yoghurt

Process raspberries in a blender until smooth. Add remaining ingredients and blend thoroughly. Pour into a paper lined loaf tin, cover and freeze for at least 4 hours. Remove from freezer 10–15 minutes before serving.

Optional: Use a variety of fresh fruit to flavour this yummy ice-cream. Bananas, strawberries, mango, blueberries, etc all roughly chopped.

Pears with Ginger Infused Chocolate

SERVES 4–6

- 500g dark chocolate, broken into pieces
- 300ml cream
- 1 tsp. Gourmet Garden Ginger
- 800g can pear halves, drained

Place chocolate in a large bowl. In a saucepan, bring cream and ginger to the boil over a medium heat, then pour over chocolate pieces. Rest for a few minutes before stirring until mixture is smooth. Divide pears among serving bowls and drizzle evenly with the chocolate.

Rockmelon Balls with Wine & Mint

SERVES 8

- 1 rockmelon (melon)
- 375ml of a rich dessert wine
- 2 tbs. caster sugar
- 1 tsp. Gourmet Garden Mint

Cut a rockmelon in half and remove the seeds. With a melon baller, scoop out as many balls as possible. Place them in a bowl. In a separate bowl, mix dessert wine (try a Muscat or riesling) with sugar until dissolved, stir in mint. Pour over the rockmelon balls; mix carefully taking care not to damage the balls. Cover and refrigerate for 2 hours before tossing to serve.

Optional: Delicious with creamy vanilla ice-cream.

Mint & Raspberry Rocky Road

SERVES 4–6

- *250g milk chocolate*
- *100g macadamia nuts, roughly chopped*
- *200g pkt Raspberries (jelly lollies)*
- *1 tbs. Gourmet Garden Mint, brought to room temperature*

Break chocolate into pieces and melt in microwave on medium high stirring every 20 seconds. Allow to cool slightly before stirring through remaining ingredients. Mix until well combined. Line a small rectangular dish with baking paper, pour the mixture in, neaten edges and refrigerate until set. Cut into desired serving pieces.

Rosemary Baked Bananas

SERVES 4

The combination of these flavours makes this dish a success.

- *4 bananas*
- *1 tsp. Gourmet Garden Rosemary*
- *400g can Carnation caramel*

Preheat oven to 200°C. Create four squares of foil 30cm in size. Peel the bananas and place in the centre of each piece of foil. Lightly rub with rosemary before wrapping securely. Place the parcels on a baking tray and bake for 10–12 minutes. Meanwhile melt half a tin of caramel until it is a nice runny consistency. Take the bananas out of the foil and split lengthways, arrange on a serving plate and drizzle with the caramel.

Sweet Red Chilli with Mango

SERVES 4

Yummy served with a scoop of creamy vanilla ice-cream.

- *1 tsp. Gourmet Garden Chilli*
- *½ cup (100g) caster sugar*
- *½ lemon, juiced*
- *2 large, ripe mangoes*

In a saucepan, place chilli, sugar, lemon juice and 1¼ cups (300ml) of water. Bring to the boil over medium heat, then simmer gently for 20 minutes or until syrupy. Transfer to a bowl and refrigerate. Arrange the slices of mango on a serving plate and spoon over the sweet chilli syrup.

For the Children

One of the best things you can teach a child is a love of food and how to cook. They will learn a lifelong skill and you might even get a hand with the washing up!

Chocolate Mint Mousse

MAKES 4

- *125g milk chocolate, broken*
- *½ tsp. Gourmet Garden Mint*
- *4 eggs, separated*
- *50g white chocolate*

In a heatproof bowl, place the milk chocolate and mint on a saucepan of simmering water and melt. Remove from heat and cool slightly. Beat eggs yolks and slowly add them to the chocolate, stirring well. Whisk the egg whites in a mixing bowl until soft peaks form. With a spatula, gently fold into the chocolate until evenly mixed. Distribute the mixture across four small ramekins and set in the fridge for at least 2 hours. Decorate with grated white chocolate.

Tip: Children LOVE cracking eggs in the kitchen. The easiest way to have them doing this successfully is to crack the shell and pour the egg onto a saucer. Place an eggcup over the yolk and pour the white into a bowl.

Golden Chicken Nuggets

SERVES 2–4

These are requested at least twice a week!

- 1 cup (260g) whole egg mayonnaise
- ½ tsp. Gourmet Garden Basil
- 2 chicken breasts, cut into bite-size pieces
- 1 cup (130g) breadcrumbs

Preheat oven to 180°C. Mix mayonnaise and basil before coating chicken pieces in it. Roll in breadcrumbs and lay on a baking paper lined baking tray. Bake for 15 minutes or until golden brown.

Grape & Orange Salad

SERVES 4–6

- 6 oranges, 1 juiced
- 400g purple seedless grapes, washed
- 200g honey flavoured yoghurt
- ½ tsp. Gourmet Garden Mint

Peel and chop oranges removing seeds and pith. Place orange segments, grapes and juice in a bowl. Gently toss and serve drizzled with the combined yoghurt and mint.

Fish Fingers

MAKES 10

- 300g fresh fish fillets
- 1 egg, beaten
- 2 tbs. Gourmet Garden Lemon Grass
- 2 cups (100g) fresh breadcrumbs

Preheat oven to 200°C. Cut fish into fingers about 10 x 3cm pieces. Mix egg and lemongrass in a bowl. Dip each piece of fish into egg, then into breadcrumbs to coat. Lay onto a paper lined baking tray and cook for 10–15 minutes, turning halfway through. Cook until golden and crisp.

Tip: Fish is a great source of protein, vitamins and minerals, in fact all types of seafood contain omega-3 fats that help maintain a healthy heart ... Encourage your children to eat it at least weekly!

Fruit Kebabs with Honey Mint Sauce

MAKES 12

These are a hit at children's parties, healthy and heavenly!

- ½ rockmelon (melon), diced
- 1 punnet strawberries, washed and hulled
- 200g honey flavoured yoghurt
- ¼ tsp. Gourmet Garden Mint

Thread pieces of rockmelon and strawberries onto mini-bamboo skewers and lay on a serving plate. Mix together yoghurt and mint and dollop into a little side plate. Serve either on the plate as a dipping sauce or drizzled over the kebabs.

Grilled Chicken Drumsticks

SERVES 4

- *4–6 chicken legs or thighs*
- *2 tbs. olive oil*
- *3 tbs. Gourmet Garden Italian Herbs*

Rub chicken with oil and on a hot BBQ or grill plate, cook for 10 minutes. Coat each piece with Italian Herbs, brushing evenly. Continue cooking for a further 5–10 minutes or until done, turning occasionally.

Healthy Hotdogs

SERVES 4

- *4 organic sausages*
- *4 wraps*
- *2 tbs. Gourmet Garden Parsley*
- *1 cup grated cheddar cheese*

Grill or BBQ sausages. Lay wraps out, spread with parsley and sprinkle with cheese. Place sausage on top, roll up tightly and cut in half to serve.

Optional: Serve with tomato or BBQ sauce, add whatever vegetables your children will eat — asparagus is particularly nice.

Herbed Pork Mince Burgers

SERVES 4

- *500g pork mince*
- *½ small red onion, finely diced*
- *1 tbs. Gourmet Garden Italian Herbs*
- *½ cup (25g) fresh breadcrumbs*

Mix all ingredients together and season well. Divide the mixture evenly into four portions, shape each into a burger and pan fry over a medium/hot heat for 4 minutes each side or until golden brown.

Optional: Serve in a fresh baguette, with a crisp piece of lettuce and a dollop of tomato chutney.

Tip: Bread crumbs are a great way to use day-old bread.

Margarita Pizza

MAKES 2

- *2 English muffins, cut in half*
- *2 tbs. tomato paste*
- *2 tbs. Gourmet Garden Basil*
- *1 cup grated mozzarella cheese*

Preheat oven to 180°C. Onto the muffins, spread tomato paste, then basil then sprinkle with cheese. Pop into oven on a pizza tray for 8–10 minutes or until cheese is bubbling … Quick, easy and delicious!

Mini Quiches

MAKES 6

- *6 slices of bread, crusts removed*
- *1 tbs. Gourmet Garden Italian herbs*
- *50g cheddar cheese, grated*
- *6 small eggs*

Preheat oven to 200°C. Spread bread lightly with Italian Herbs. Press gently into non-stick muffin cups. Fill each cup with cheese and a sprinkle of pepper. Top each with an egg and bake for 15 minutes or until set.

Mint Choc Strawberries

MAKES 12

- *12 large ripe strawberries, washed and dry*
- *100g milk chocolate*
- *½ tsp. Gourmet Garden Mint*

In a double boiler, melt chocolate and mint until nice and smooth. Dip whole strawberries into chocolate and place on a paper lined baking tray. When all are dipped, set in the fridge.

Optional: Melt a little white chocolate and drizzle over each on the baking tray for a dazzling serving effect.

Pasta Bake

SERVES 6

Watch this fly!

- *4 cups cooked macaroni (approx. 2 cups uncooked)*
- *400g can tomato soup*
- *1 tbs. Gourmet Garden Garlic*
- *115g tasty cheese, grated*

Preheat oven to 180°C. Place macaroni, soup, garlic and a ⅓ of cheese in a large bowl and mix well before pouring into a casserole dish. Top with remaining grated cheese and bake for 20 minutes.

Optional: Add some diced bacon or ham prior to baking.

Potato Boats

SERVES 4

- *4 large potatoes (250g each)*
- *1 tsp. Gourmet Garden Chives*
- *115g ham*
- *115g cheddar cheese, grated*

Preheat oven to 200°C. Wash and dry potatoes before pricking each with a fork. Place on a baking tray and bake for 60–70 minutes or until soft inside and crispy on the outside. Cut each potato in half, scoop out 80% of the flesh. Mash the potato well, add chives and season. Place skins back onto the baking tray and evenly spread chopped ham into each, top with mashed potato and sprinkle with cheese. Cook for a further 15 minutes or until the cheese is golden on top.

Optional: For a vegie option, try some fried mushrooms instead of the ham. This is also nice with bacon or tuna.

Raspberry and Ginger Jellies

SERVES 4

- 85g pkt Raspberry flavoured jelly
- 4 ripe strawberries, diced
- ½ tsp. Gourmet Garden Ginger

Make jelly as directed on packet. Coat strawberry pieces with ginger and evenly distribute between four ½ cup sized ramekins. Over each, pour jelly. Allow to set in fridge for at least 4 hours or until firm.

Rosemary Glazed Vegetable Shapes

SERVES 2

These put a thrill into eating vegetables!

- 1 potato, peeled
- 100g piece pumpkin (butternut squash), peeled
- 2 tbs. olive oil
- ½ tsp. Gourmet Garden Rosemary

Preheat oven to 180°C. Slice potato and pumpkin into 2cm thick slices. Using metal shapes like stars, hearts and animal shapes cut out as many shapes as possible. Baste with the combined mixture of oil and rosemary and bake for 15–20 minutes, turning halfway through.

Optional: Keep scraps and make a mashed potato and pumpkin on another night.

Sausage Rolls

MAKES 20

- 1 carrot, peeled and grated
- 1 tbs. Gourmet Garden Parsley
- 250g chicken mince
- 2 sheets ready rolled puff pastry

Preheat oven to 180°C. Line a baking tray with baking paper. Combine carrot, mince and parsley, season and mix well. Slice the sheet of pastry in half. Place a portion of mince on the middle of the long-edge of the pastry and pat the mince into a long sausage shape. Brush the sides of the pastry with water, and roll it over to seal. Do this as firmly as possible so the pastry is neat and tight. Cut each roll into 5. Place on baking tray about 2cm apart. Bake for 20 minutes or until the pastry is puffy and the mince is cooked through.

Optional: Brush the top of the pastry with egg or milk prior to baking.

Spaghetti Bolognaise

SERVES 6

- 400g spaghetti
- 400g lean mince
- 425g jar organic pasta sauce
- 1 tbs. Gourmet Garden Italian Herbs

Boil spaghetti to manufacturer's instructions. Add mince to a non-stick frying pan and heat until brown. Pour in pasta sauce and Italian herbs and simmer together for 5 minutes. Serve the mince over drained spaghetti.

Optional: Sprinkle with lashings of fresh parmesan cheese.

Tuna & Parsley Cakes

SERVES 2

- 500g potatoes, peeled, cooked and mashed
- 185g tuna, drained
- ½ cup grated carrot
- 1 tbs. Gourmet Garden Parsley

Into the saucepan of mashed potatoes add remaining ingredients. Season with sea salt and pepper then fold ingredients together until well combined. Using a ¼ cup measurement shape patties using your hands. Heat a large non-stick frying pan, and cook patties until golden brown.

Watermelon Ice-blocks

MAKES 12

- ½ cup (110g) sugar
- ½ tsp. Gourmet Garden Mint
- 2 tbs. fresh lemon juice
- 1 kg seedless watermelon, cut into chunks

Place 1 cup (250ml) of water and sugar into a medium sized saucepan. Over medium heat stir until sugar dissolves. Add mint and bring to the boil. Boil for 5 minutes or until mixture thickens slightly. Remove from heat and strain into a small bowl, chill for 10 minutes. Pop syrup, watermelon and lemon juice into a blender and blend until smooth. Pour mixture evenly into ice-block moulds, seal with lids and freeze for at least 3 hours prior to serving.

Drinks

Herbs and spices provide a multitude of health benefits.

Look beyond food to include them in your daily diet. You can use a variety of flavours to make fabulous herb and spice-enhanced coolers, spritzers, mocktails, smoothies, teas and ades.

This refreshing list of drinks is just a sample of what can be created with a little imagination and a few herbal flavours.

Apple Ginger & Mint

SERVES 4

- *8 large Granny Smith apples, chopped and cored*
- *1 tbs. freshly squeezed lemon juice*
- *1 tbs. Gourmet Garden Ginger*
- *½ cup fresh mint leaves, chopped*

Juice apples, add remaining ingredients, blend and serve over a glass of crushed ice.

Tip: Mint is packed with many vitamins and minerals. So if you have any leftover, relish this herb by cutting the leaves into minute portions to use as a garnish.

Banana & Rosemary Frappé

SERVES 2

- *1 cup pineapple juice*
- *2 bananas, sliced*
- *1 tbs. honey*
- *½ tsp. Gourmet Garden Rosemary*

Combine all ingredients in a blender with 1 cup of ice, and puree until smooth.

Energiser Drink

SERVES 1

- *1 carrot, peeled*
- *½ tsp. Gourmet Garden Ginger*
- *2 celery stalks*
- *1 orange, peeled*

Juice all ingredients and serve over crushed ice.

Homemade Lemonade

MAKES 1 LITRE

- *1 cup (200g) caster sugar*
- *1 cup (250ml) lemon juice*
- *1 tbs. Gourmet Garden Lemon Grass*
- *3 cups (750ml) soda water, chilled*

Place the caster sugar in a saucepan with 1 cup water and stir over low heat until the sugar dissolves. Allow to cool. Stir in the lemon juice and lemon grass. To serve, add chilled soda water and lots of crushed ice.

Kiwi & Mint Frappé

SERVES 2

- *4 kiwifruits (340g), peeled, chopped coarsely*
- *¼ cup (60ml) apple juice*
- *½ tsp. Gourmet Garden Mint*
- *1 tsp. caster sugar*

Blend or process all ingredients with 1 cup of ice until well combined. Pour into glasses to serve.

Optional: Garnish with some shredded mint.

Minty Apple Iced Tea

MAKES 1 LITRE

- *3 peppermint tea bags*
- *2 cups (500ml) apple juice*
- *½ tsp. Gourmet Garden Mint*
- *1 small crunchy apple, thinly sliced*

Soak teabags in 2 cups (500ml) boiling water and stand for 10 minutes. Discard bags. Pour tea into a jug, mix in juice and mint. Cover with food wrap and chill for an hour before serving in tall glasses over plenty of ice. Add apple slices, stir and serve.

Optional: Blend the ingredients with ½ a cup of ice and pour into a large glass.

Orange, Lemon & Strawberry Juice

MAKES 1

- 2 oranges
- 1 lemon
- 1 cup strawberries
- 1 tsp. Gourmet Garden Lemon Grass

Peel oranges and lemon and quarter. Remove seeds, add strawberries, lemon grass and 6 cubes of ice and blend. This is a great *'fresh start to the day'* juice.

Pina Colada Shake

MAKES 4

- 1 pineapple, peeled, cut and juiced
- 1 cup (250ml) coconut milk
- 2 bananas, sliced
- 1 tsp. Gourmet Garden Mint

Combine all ingredients in a blender with 1 cup of ice and process until smooth.

Pineapple & Mint Juice

MAKES 2

- 1 pineapple, peeled and cut
- 1 tsp. Gourmet Garden Mint

Blend well and serve chilled over crushed ice.

Strawberry & Basil Smoothie

MAKES 2

- 1 cup (250ml) chilled organic apple juice (if more than 90% juice, or 4 apples)
- 2 ripe bananas, sliced
- 1 tbs. Gourmet Garden Basil
- 1 punnet chilled strawberries, washed and hulled

Blend all ingredients together and serve chilled ... YUM!

Watermelon & Ginger Crush

SERVES 4

- 1 kg seedless watermelon, cut into chunks
- ¼ cup fresh mint leaves
- 2 tbs. caster sugar
- 1 tsp. Gourmet Garden Ginger

Place watermelon in a blender and blend until smooth. Add 2 cups of ice and remaining ingredients and blend until the ice is crushed. Taste and add more ginger if needed. Pour into tall glasses, garnish with extra mint leaves and serve.

Optional: Substitute fresh mint for 1 tbs. Gourmet Garden Mint.

Herbs & Spices Matched & Married

We have included this table based on the extensive research and cooking we did compiling this book. It suggests seasonings for a variety of foods. Its purpose is to provide a helpful guide. Naturally, it is up to you to experiment with the foods and flavours best suited to the tastes and diets of you and your family ... Enjoy!

FOOD	SEASONING
Beef	Bay leaf, cayenne pepper, chilli, curry, dill, ginger, mustard, paprika, marjoram, oregano, parsley, rosemary, thyme.
Pork	Allspice, apple, basil, cardamom, cinnamon, cloves, curry, ginger, marjoram, mustard, oregano, paprika, parsley, rosemary, sage, savory, thyme.
Lamb	Basil, cardamom, curry, dill, mace, marjoram, mint, oregano, paprika, rosemary, turmeric.
Poultry	Allspice, anise, bay leaf, cayenne, curry, dill, ginger, marjoram, mustard, nutmeg, paprika, parsley, pepper, sage, savory, tarragon, thyme.
Fish	Allspice, anise, basil, bay leaf, cayenne, chives, curry, dill, fennel, ginger, marjoram, nutmeg, oregano, paprika, parsley, tarragon, thyme.
Fruit	Allspice, anise, cinnamon, cloves, curry, ginger, mace, mint, nutmeg.
Desserts	Allspice, basil, chilli, cinnamon, ginger, mint, nutmeg, zests of citrus fruits.
Beans	Dill, marjoram, nutmeg, oregano.
Beetroot	Allspice, honey, nutmeg.
Broccoli	Garlic, mustard, nutmeg, sage.
Carrots	Coriander, dill, garlic, ginger, honey, nutmeg, parsley, rosemary, thyme.
Cucumbers	Basil, dill, parsley.
Eggplant (aubergine)	Garlic, mint, oregano, parsley.
Mushrooms	Garlic, sage, tarragon.
Peas	Garlic, marjoram, mint, sage.
Potatoes	Chives, cumin, dill, fennel, garlic, mace, parsley, rosemary, tarragon.
Squash	Cardamom, ginger, nutmeg.
Tomato	Allspice, basil, cloves, cumin, fennel, marjoram, oregano, parsley.
Rice	Chives, cumin, curry, nutmeg, parsley, saffron, turmeric.

Biography

Kim McCosker

Kim was born in Stanthorpe and raised in Mundubbera. Schooled on the Gold Coast, completing a Bachelor of International Finance, Kim trained with MLC as a Financial Planner completing her Diploma in Financial Planning through Deakin University. Kim's natural ease with people, her ability to communicate effortlessly and her relaxed confidence served her well as a successful financial adviser and later as the Queensland State Manager of MLC Private Client Services. Kim worked for 7 years in the finance industry before finally resigning to spend the time raising her beautiful boys.

It was during this phase of her life that **4 Ingredients** was born. Kim had the idea for some time, but it was at the suggestion of her lifelong friend Rachael Bermingham they write it. Taking a year to compile and cook, **4 Ingredients** (or Kim's fourth child as she lovingly refers to it) was born in March, 2007. From an initial print run of 2,000 that were *"never going to sell"* Kim and Rachael went onto orchestrate what the trade now refers to as *'An absolute phenomenon!'* Having now sold over 3 million copies of their titles, filmed 2 TV series for the Lifestyle Channel (broadcast into 12 countries worldwide), produced an iTunes App called 4 Ingredients, they are working on a fabulous version for the Apple iPad, have launched a unique cookware range and are developing a debut supermarket line. The future is very exciting and when asked about it Kim happily shares, *"The aim is to continue building a dynamic enterprise that not only we, but Australia is very proud of."*

But of all that has been accomplished, the most rewarding by far has been the birth of her three precious boys Morgan 8, Hamilton 5 and Flynn 2. For Kim, *family is the most important thing* in the world and with the loving support of her wonderful husband Glen, she is able to juggle the demands of a busy work life around her treasured home life. Life presents many opportunities, but having the courage and the time to purse them, in what is an ever increasingly busy and demanding world, is hard. But Kim is living proof that you can achieve whatever you want in life with *a great idea* and **lots of HARD WORK!**

You can contact Kim by:
E info@4ingredients.com.au   *O +61 (7) 5341 8282*
W www.4ingredients.co.uk   *W www.4ingredients.com.au*

Biography

Rachael Bermingham

Rachael Bermingham (nee Moore) was born in Stanthorpe on Queensland's Darling Downs.

Always seeking adventure, Rachael trained to become one of 3 women in Australia to professionally feed sharks at Underwater World which she did for 3 years, was a state champion in martial arts, and even did a small stint as a stuntwoman at Warner Brothers Movie World.

An energetic, dynamic and proud mum to 3 gorgeous little boys (including 9 week old twins), Rachael has written 6 bestselling books in the last 4 years and is regarded as one of Australia's #1 female self-published authors.

Rachael co-wrote, self-published and self-funded her 1st book *'Read My Lips'* in 2005 (a motivational book for women on how to achieve their goals) while breastfeeding her son Jaxson, before being asked to utilise her book writing experience and marketing talent and embark on another exciting authoring venture with life long friend Kim McCosker to write what has become the phenomenally successful **4 Ingredients** cookbook series. Rachael released her 5th and first solo title *'How to write your own book and make it a bestseller'* which also became an overnight bestseller.

A natural entrepreneur, Rachael's talent for business shone early on when she succeeded in opening her first business at the tender age of 19 (a hair salon). In her 20 years in business she has become most renowned for her ability and natural flair in building multi-million dollar companies from a home base around family commitments with clever 'no cost' marketing and business tactics coupled with effective time management and goal setting strategies.

Her passion for helping others to succeed and transform their goals into achievements eventually evolved in the form of authoring books, speaking, and mentoring women in six different countries.

When Rachael's not working on new books, mentoring, speaking or whipping up something fabulous in the kitchen she can be found enjoying what she loves most; 'chillaxing' at home with her fabulous friends and family soaking up the spectacular sun, surf and sand of Queensland's beautiful Sunshine Coast in Australia.

Bibliography

Books

Shipard Isabel. **How can I use HERBS in my daily life?** PO Box 66, Nambour, QLD 4560 Australia. Published by Dave Stewart 2003.

Farrow Joanna. **Herbs.** 88–89 Blackfriars Road. London SE1 8HA. Hermes House, an imprint of Anness Publishing LTD, 2001.

Castleman Michael. **The New Healing Herbs.** Rodale Inc. USA, 2009.

Cox Jeff, Moine Marie-Pierre. **The Cook's Herb Garden.** DK Limited (Penguin) 80 The Strand, London, WC20RL. 2010

Gwyther Pamela. **Let's Cook.** Queen Street House. 4 Queen Street. Bath BA1 1HE, UK. Parragon Books Ltd, 2008.

Company's Coming. **Kids' Healthy Cooking.** 45–55 Fairchild Street, Heatherton Victoria 3202 Australia. Hinkler Books Pty Ltd, 2009.

Lloyd Susan. **Dinner Party Cookbook.** 169 Phillip Street, Waterloo, N.S.W. Australia. Australian Universities Press Pty Ltd, 1974.

Australian Table. **The Origins of Mandarins.** Ylla Wright. March 2005.

The Australian Womens Weekly Cookbooks. **Great Vegetarian Food.** Sydney, Australia. ACP Publishing Pty Ltd, 2001.

Super Food Ideas. **Best Ever Super-Fast 98 Family Favourites.** 170–180 Bourke Road, Alexandria NSW 2015. News Magazines 2009.

Australian Women's Health. May, June & July 2010. Published by Pacific Magazines Pty Ltd. 8 Central Avenue, Everleigh, NSW 2015

McCosker Kim, Bermingham Rachael, **4 Ingredients Fast Fresh & Healthy** PO Box 400, Caloundra QLD 4551. Published by: 4 Ingredients Books, 2007.

Bibliography

Webpages

Making Herbs & Spices Easy for Everyday Cooking
http://www.gourmetgarden.com.au

Find your inner Chef with our recipe search
http://www.gourmetgarden.com.au

Healing Through Natural Herbs Explained
http://www.womens-health-fitness.com/healing-through-natural-herbs.html

Herbs & Spices for Every Kitchen
http://www.thehomeherbalist.com/herbs-and-spices-for-every-kitchen/

Herbs and Spices what goes with what foods? 13/06/2007
http://ag.udel.edu/extension/fnutri/pdf/CookingGuide/fnf-13.pdf

Mint Health Benefits. March 9, 2009.
http://www.greenherbalremedies.com/blog/mint-health-benefits

An Australian Government, State and Territory health initiative.
"Why 2 & 5."
http://www.gofor2and5.com.au/

Seven nutritional benefits of eating lamb.
http://library.thinkquest.org/CR0215162/meat.html

Interesting Pork Facts. October 2008.
www.askthemeatman.com/interesting_pork_facts.htm

Index

Foreword 3

Fresh Made Easy 4

Guide to Weights & Measures 6

Abbreviations Used 7

Oven Temperature Guide 7

4 Ingredients Titles 8

Table of Contents 9

Breakfasts 11

    Breakfast Tomatoes 11
    Ham, Basil & Feta Scrambled Eggs 12
    Herbed Cream Cheese Omelette 12
    Fluffy Scrambled Eggs with Chives 13
    Garlic Hash Browns 13
    Ginger Pancakes 14
    Ginger & Tomato Jam 14
    Individual Egg Bakes 15
    Mango Mint Smoothie 16
    Marmalade 16
    Parsley Omelette 17
    Savoury Egg in a Hole 17

Dips 18

    Avocado Cups 18
    Basil Pesto Dip 18
    Corn Chips 19
    Creamy Dill & Feta Spread 19
    Garlic Roasted Pepper Dip 20
    Moroccan Hummus 20
    Pumpkin & Basil Dip 21
    Rosemary Parmesan Biscuits 21
    Salmon Pat´ 22
    Tapenade 22
    Zucchini & Chive Dip 23

Condiments 24

    Aioli 24
    Asian Dipping Sauce 24
    Balsamic & Garlic Dressing 25
    Chilli Dipping Sauce 25
    Dill Yoghurt Dressing 26
    Herbal Fruit Salad Dressing 26
    Mango & Coriander Salsa 27
    Mint Sauce 27
    Parsley & Lemon Salad Dressing 28
    Parsley Vinaigrette 28
    Peanut, Chilli, Coriander & Lime Salsa 29
    Red Wine & Garlic Gravy 29
    Satay Sauce 30
    Thai Dressing 30

Cocktail Food 31

Brie & Quince Matchsticks 31
Brie Bruschetta 32
BBQ Garlic Prawns 32
Cheese & Coriander Quesadillas 33
Chorizo with Parsley & Olives 33
Green Eyed Pickles 34
Marinated & Baked Olives 34
Minted Lamb Balls 35
Oysters with Mango Chilli 35
Prosciutto Wrapped Haloumi 36
Salmon Blinis 36
Thai Chicken Balls 37

Morning & Afternoon Teas 38

Almond & Ginger Stuffed Dates 38
Chocolate Chilli Lychees 38
Chocolate Stacks 39
Coconut & Mint Balls 39
Date & Ginger Loaf 40
Ginger Macaroons 40
Fruit Cake 41
Fruit Mint Palmiers 41
Fruit Slice 42
Jam Tarts 42
Rosemary Shortbread 43
White Choc Chilli Macadamias 43

Light Meals & Lunches 44

Beef & Basil Baguette 44
Chorizo & Potato Frittata 45
Chilli Chicken Wings 45
Ham and Egg Quiches 46
Lemon Grass & Chicken Soup 46
Pumpkin, Ginger & Garlic Soup 47
Roasted Tomato & Basil Soup 47
Sausage Rolls 48
Spicy BBQ Calamari 48
Summer Thai BBQ Prawns 49
Thai Beef Koftas 49
Toasted French Bread 50
Zucchini, Leek & Mint Soup 50

Sides 51

Salads 51

Asparagus with Thai Dressing 51
Carrot & Walnut Salad 52
Curried Eggs 52
Garden Salad 53
Pea & Feta Salad 53
Potato Salad 54
Tomato & Bocconcini Salad 54
Warm Mediterranean Salad 55

Potato 56

Basil Baked Potatoes 56
Double Baked Chive Potatoes 57

Garlic Mash...57
Hot Chilli Mash...58
Mashed Sweet Potatoes...58
Potato Bake...59
Roasted Potatoes with Lemon & Garlic 59
Rosemary & Thyme Roasted Potatoes...60
Sweet Potato & Beetroot Wedges..61
Wedges with Garlic & Rosemary 61

Vegetables...62

BBQ Corn with Italian Herbs...62
Caramelized Zucchini with Mint..63
Garlic Mushrooms..63
Ginger & Coriander Carrots..64
Italian Peas..64
Minted Lemon Asparagus..65
Minty Peas 65
Oven Baked Tomatoes...66
Rosemary & Garlic Roasted Pumpkin...66
Sautéed Mushrooms...67
Snow Peas in Garlic Mint Butter 67
Spinach with Garlic...68
Zucchini Pesto Sticks...68

Mains 69

Beef 69

Basil & Parmesan Steaks 69
Beef Curry..70
Garlic Pepper Steak...70
Moroccan Stew...71
Prosciutto Wrapped Veal...71
Rissoles 72
Roast Beef..72
Spicy Steak...73
Steak with Mushroom & Garlic Sauce 73
Steak Burgundy..74
Thai Beef Stir-Fry..74

Chicken...75

Asian Chicken...75
Chilli & Lime Chicken Wings...76
Creamy Chives & Garlic Chicken..76
Garlic & Rosemary Baked Chicken...77
Herb Infused Roast Chicken..78
Honey & Lime Baked Drumsticks...79
Mediterranean Chicken...79
Sweet & Spicy Chicken...80
Thai Chicken & Cashew Stir-fry..80

Fish & Seafood 81

Baked Salmon with Parmesan Crust..81
BBQ Marinated Calamari 82
Creamy Garlic Prawns..82
Malaysian Fish Curry..83
Maple & Mustard Glazed Salmon 83
Mediterranean Baked Fish..84
Minted Apricot Fish 84

Moroccan Salmon 85
Mussels in White Wine 85
Prawn & Chorizo Skewers...86
Salmon & Herbs in Prosciutto Parcels 86
Steamed Garlic Mussels 87
Steamed Ginger Snapper 87
Stir-Fried Prawns 88

Lamb 89

Balsamic Glazed Lamb Cutlets 89
Greek Style Roast Lamb 90
Lamb Racks with Mustard Glaze 90
Lamb & Mint Patties 91
Mediterranean Char-Grilled Lamb 91
Moroccan Lamb with Shiraz and Honey Sauce 92
Moroccan Lamb Koftas..93
Roast Lamb 93

Pasta 94

Crab Spaghetti..94
Garlic Bread 95
Greek Spaghetti 95
Lemon Pepper Pasta 96
Matriciana 96
Mediterranean Prawn Linguini..97
Pasta with Crab & Lemon Cream Sauce 97
Quick Pasta Sauce 98
Ricotta Spaghetti 98
Marinara Sauce..99
Spinach Garlic Pasta 99
Spaghetti Al Olio 100
Spaghetti with Garlic & Basil...100

Pork 101

BBQ Spare Ribs...101
Dill & Honey Pork Chops...102
Grilled Sausages with Tomato Stew 102
Italian Style Pork Chops 103
Mediterranean Grilled Sausages 103
Orange & Ginger Glaze 104
Pork & Potatoes in Red Wine...104
Roast Pork...105
San Choy Bow 105

Vegetarian Mains...106

Asparagus & Lemon Risotto 106
Baked Potato with Tomato Salsa 107
Baked Ravioli 107
Corn & Chives Frittatas..108
Gourmet Pizza 108
Herbed Potato Frittatas...109
Pasta with Basil...109
Pea & Mint Omelette...110
Polenta Chips 110
Thai Chickpea Patties 111
Thai Green Curry...111
Tuscan Stuffed Peppers...112

Desserts...113

Almond Brittle with Rosemary 113
Basil & Lime Syrup 114
Caramel Tart 114
Chocolate & Basil Ganache 115
Choc-Mint Candied Peel..115
Lychees in Mint & Ginger Syrup 116
Raspberry Mint Soft Serve..116
Pears with Ginger Infused Chocolate........................117
Rockmelon Balls with Wine & Mint 117
Mint & Raspberry Rocky Road 118
Rosemary Baked Bananas 118
Sweet Red Chilli with Mango 119

For the Children 120

Chocolate Mint Mousse 120
Golden Chicken Nuggets 121
Grape & Orange Salad 121
Fish Fingers 122
Fruit Kebabs with Honey Mint Sauce 122
Grilled Chicken Drumsticks..123
Healthy Hotdogs 123
Herbed Pork Mince Burgers...124
Margarita Pizza 124
Mini Quiches 125
Mint Choc Strawberries 125
Pasta Bake 126
Potato Boats..126
Raspberry and Ginger Jellies 127
Rosemary Glazed Vegetable Shapes..........................127
Sausage Rolls 128
Spaghetti Bolognaise 128
Tuna & Parsley Cakes...129
Watermelon Ice-blocks...129

Drinks 130

Apple Ginger & Mint 130
Banana & Rosemary Frappé 131
Energiser Drink..131
Homemade Lemonade 131
Kiwi & Mint Frappé 132
Minty Apple Iced Tea..132
Orange, Lemon & Strawberry Juice 133
Pina Colada Shake 133
Pineapple & Mint Juice 133
Strawberry & Basil Smoothie.......................................134
Watermelon & Ginger Crush 134

Herbs & Spices Matched & Married 135

Biography 136

Kim McCosker..136
Rachael Bermingham...137

Bibliography 138

Books 138
Webpages 139